Understanding Organizational

Behavior

THE DORSEY SERIES IN ANTHROPOLOGY
AND SOCIOLOGY

EDITORS

PETER H. ROSSI
University of Chicago

WILLIAM FOOTE WHYTE
Cornell University

ARGYRIS   *Understanding Organizational Behavior*

ADAMS & PREISS (eds.)   *Human Organization Research*   (Published for the Society for Applied Anthropology)

Understanding Organizational Behavior

By CHRIS ARGYRIS

Associate Professor of Industrial Administration
Yale University

1960

THE DORSEY PRESS, INC. · HOMEWOOD, ILLINOIS

To my brothers

PETER AND TOM

Preface

FROM TIME to time it is useful to pause to organize one's present views, to evaluate one's progress (or lack of it), and, as a result, to plan the future research more effectively. It is important to obtain the assistance of others in this endeavor because my ego-involvement prevents me from seeing clearly all the gaps and weaknesses (and perhaps even some strengths) of the present approach. It is hoped that some of the readers will be kind enough to communicate their constructive criticisms and make suggestions for new directions. In return this work is offered with the hope that it may stimulate ideas that will soon outdate those found herein or, at the very least, prevent others from making similar errors.

A second important motivation to write this work is related to the great increase of requests that behavioral scientists are receiving, especially from high-level administrators in industry, government, and education to describe more concretely (1) how they conduct research in an organization, (2) the requirements of research upon the participants, and finally (3) the advantages that might accrue from the research to the organization. Although this is written primarily for the researcher, it is hoped that the operating executive, and especially his staff advisors in this area, might find it helpful. In stating this hope, I want to emphasize that this work by no means represents the richness of viewpoints that exist today on how to diagnose organizational behavior. It represents only one man's point of view—and one that is just beginning to evolve. The book therefore is best seen as an interim report rather than as a completed, final presentation.

The plan for the presentation is a relatively simple one. In Chapter I the main themes are the focus of the research, the research strategy, the theoretical model, and the methodological guideposts found necessary to supplement the theoretical framework which is still in its infancy.

In Chapter II the actual research procedures are discussed in detail. It takes up the role of the researcher, the type of interview, the research strategy underlying the questions used, and the primary and secondary objectives of each question. The chapter closes with a detailed discussion of the interview situation. The physical setting, overcoming the social distance between the researcher and the respondent, notetaking during the interview, explaining the research to each respondent, the methods respondents tend to use to cope with the researcher, the problems of maintaining a professional role, and dealing with the reticent respondent are examples of the topics discussed.

A concrete example (called Plant X) is presented in Chapter III to show how the theory and the method are used in diagnosing a particular organization. The focus of the diagnoses are upon the mechanisms of how the systems maintains itself. In Chapter IV we attempt to show how the model of Plant X's social system helps one to begin to understand more systematically the problems of quantifying individual and organizational actualization and to make predictions about how crucial parts of the system will react to changes. The model developed for Plant X is then used in Chapter V to make *a priori* predictions about a new plant (Y). More specifically hypotheses are derived from the model of the Plant X as to (1) the differences one will find between Plant X and Y and (2) within Plant Y (among different departments). Chapter VI is a discussion of some of the important unanswered questions regarding the theory and the method.

Finally in Chapter VII we describe some of the positive results of the research as seen by the practitioner. Although the book is not directed toward the operating executive, he and the interested researcher may find it of interest to see how one series of studies was found useful by the administrators and the researcher.

As always, I am deeply indebted to many people. First there are the participants in Plant X and Y who co-operated so enthusiastically with the study. Next, I should like to express my appreciation to the National Institutes of Mental Health (3M–

9128) for the financial aid. Dr. Raymond Gould of NIMH was especially helpful in helping me clarify my views and in providing other kinds of moral and administrative support. The committee appointed to act as advisors has been most helpful. They are Professors Gerald Caplan, George C. Homans, Robert Kaplan, David McClelland, William F. Whyte, and Warren Vaughan. Also, Professor Whyte, as consulting editor, gave me many helpful suggestion regarding the organization and presentation of the material. Professors Robert Tannenbaum and Warren Bennis took the trouble to send me most helpful discussions of their feelings about the manuscript. I have benefited from discussions with Professors E. W. Bakke and Donald W. Taylor. Some advanced students read through the early stages of the manuscript. Especially helpful were Bruce MacLeod, Harold Oaklander, Charles Brodigan, and William Tilley, Jr. Mrs. David Connolly and Miss Elizabeth McIntyre suffered through my handwriting to type the manuscript. My wife Renee spent many hours editing the manuscript as well as living through some of the emotional pangs experienced by the researcher.

CHRIS ARGYRIS

YALE UNIVERSITY
February, 1960

Table of Contents

xi

CONTENTS

CHAPTER

I

The Theory and Method

HUMAN BEINGS are need-fulfilling, goal-achieving unities.[1] They create various types of strategies to fulfill their needs and to achieve their goals. One of the most important strategies is to organize themselves.

There are several strategies by which human effort may be organized. Historically, the most frequently used strategy seems to be the one which results in a pyramid-shaped structure usually called the "formal organization." There exists now much research to show that this strategy will tend to be modified as the organization exists through a period of time.[2] Consequently the structure of the organization will change from the one represented by the pyramid shape to one which is much more complex.

The Focus of the Research

The research of the writer is directed at understanding (and consequently predicting and controlling) the behavior in organizations that initially begins with or includes at least two sets of variables; the formal organization and the individual. Schools, churches, industrial plants, banks, governmental agencies,

---

[1] In my opinion it is important that needs conceptualized to exist within the personality be also represented in the environment through the concept of goals. This implies, as Lewin, Sullivan, Fromm, May, Rogers, and others that behavior is a function of the individual and the situation (environment) in which he is imbedded. See Andras Angyal, *Foundation for a Science of Personality* (New York: Commonwealth Fund, 1941), especially pp. 88–123.

[2] For a summary of this research see Chris Argyris, *Personality and Organization* (New York: Harper & Bros., 1957).

1

trade-unions, hospitals, and the military are but a few examples. The objective of the research is to create generalizations and theory applicable to all organizations of the types defined above as well as to any given empirical case.

The requirement of understanding the uniqueness of a given case and yet generalizing to the total class raises difficult problems. The problem is particularly vexing for scientists studying organization-type phenomena. In biology, for example, research with a specific organism is designed in order that it does not violate the properties that are unique to that particular organism as well as properties that are generalizable to a class of phenomena represented by the organism. The student of social organization faces similar problems.

This leads the writer to believe that social scientists studying organizations may find it useful to examine the research methods of scientists who study living organizations (e.g., biologists). In making this suggestion, the writer is not suggesting a wholesale borrowing of biological models. Rather, the emphasis is upon borrowing a few major concepts and parts of the conceptual and research strategies used by biologists. In the next few pages some of these concepts and strategies are examined. A thorough discussion must await the existence of empirical research which, in the final analyses, will provide the best clues as to what can be borrowed from other fields of inquiry.

Living and Nonliving Organizations

A word about the meaning of living organizations. A molecule is an organized system and so is an atom. But these are not living organisms. As Russell points out, a living organism is characterized by "the weaving together in one cyclical process of the master functions of maintenance and development." [3] Underlying these characteristics is the general directiveness of its activities. By "directive activity" is meant that all the activity of a living organization is related to such objectives as self-maintenance and development. [4]

---

[3] E. S. Russell, *The Study of Behavior* (Rep. Brit. Ass., 1934), pp. 83–98.

[4] E. S. Russell, *The Directiveness of Organic Activities* (Cambridge University Press, 1946), pp. 3–5.

These properties of living organisms lead to some fundamental differences in research objectives and thinking between those studying living (biological or social) and those studying nonliving organisms. One of these differences, namely, interest in understanding the unique event is discussed in a symposium report of an eminent group of biologists entitled "Concepts in Biology." [5] For example:

I don't want to single out the chemists, so I'll say something about physicists. I have had a number of conferences within the last two years with physicists who have become intensely interested in the subject of evolution. . . . Well, in these discussions it has become very clear to me that the thinking of physicists is, on the whole, exceedingly different from that of biologists who work in the evolutionary field. The physicist finds it difficult to comprehend the uniqueness of so much that happens in biology, whether it is individuals, species, or certain biological events in animal behavior, ecology, and so forth. . . . I remember a discussion I had with the physicist W. Pauli in which, somehow or other, he just couldn't get a particular point when I spoke of a gas as having such-and-such properties, until he finally said: "Oh, you're talking about individual gases!" As soon as he got that, he got my reasoning.

A second difference is that the student of the nonliving organisms may be able to understand his "wholes" by focusing on the parts of the whole and their relationships to one another. "A thorough understanding of hydrogen atoms and oxygen atoms, plus an awareness of how such atoms are disposed in a molecule of water, should certainly lead to the inference that molecules of water would have just a middling attraction for one another and would therefore constitute, in quantity, a liquid." [6] No additional explanation is necessary. The student of living organization, however, must also relate this to objectives or to the "directiveness" of the organization.

J. S. Haldane makes this point when he states, "When we endeavor to treat physiological phenomena as separate events, we can only reach unintelligible chaos to which there is no end. When we seek to understand them as manifestations of like re-

---

[5] R. W. Gerard (ed.), "Concepts in Biology," *Behavioral Science*, Vol. III, No. 2 (April, 1958).

[6] Kendon Smith, "The Naturalistic Conception of Life," *American Science*, Vol. XLVI, No. 4 (December, 1958), p. 416.

garded as a whole, we find that we can make them intelligible and predictable." [7] Pittendrigh also states that organization is relative to an end, it differs from mere order in this respect.[8] The directiveness toward these objectives is not teleological nor does it require vitalistic or teleologic concepts. It is a property of the system. It is part of life.[9]

"Respect" for Complexity

For many years the Galilean research philosophy has been (and continues to be) the most frequently used model for many social scientists. One of its basic characteristics is the simplification of complexity. One does not study rain or leaves dropping, etc. In a bold stroke of genuis Galileo realized that one should study cannon balls rolling down an inclined plane! This is an excellent approach—when it works. And it works for many problems. But it also fails to work for many other problems.[10]

In the writer's view, the Galilean research philosophy tends to fail in the study of complexity which cannot be broken down into parts and then "added" again into a whole. The reason that the complexity related to living organization cannot be broken down is that it exists only when all of its components are in proper relationship to one another.

The "respect" for complexity is crucial in the study of the total organization. As Ashby points out:

Science has . . . for two hundred years . . . tried primarily to find, within the organism whatever is *simple*. The same strategy—of looking for the simple part—has been used incessantly in physics and chemistry. Their triumphs have been chiefly those of identifying the units out of which complex structures made. . . .

---

[7] J. S. Haldane, *The Philosophical Bases of Biology* (London, 1931), pp. 76–84.

[8] Cohen S. Pittendrigh, "Adaptation, Natural Selection and Behavior," in Anne Roe and George G. Simpson (eds.), *Behavior and Evolution* (New Haven: Yale University Press, 1958), p. 394.

[9] For a thoughtful discussion on the differences between "mechanistic" and "organismic" viewpoints see Morton Beckner, *The Biological Way of Thought* (Columbia University Press, 1959), p. 394.

[10] The writer is indebted to Professor E. Pollard, Head, Biophysics Department, Yale University, for this insight.

Later Ashby writes:

Thus Fisher initiated a new scientific strategy. Faced with a system of great complexity, he accepted complexity as an essential, a nonignorable property. . . .[11]

The student of social organization who believes that it is possible to understand organizations by breaking down their complexity into smaller and more manageable units may find unexpected long-range difficulties. Such a research strategy is based on the assumption that the organization will be understood when the results of the separate experiments are finally added together or synthesized.[12] Is this "synthesis" or "additiveness" possible? Turning again to biologists who have been studying organisms we note that Paul A. Weiss believes that organization is not something one can understand by synthesizing the results of several carefully controlled experiments (that focused on parts of an organization). Organization may be something which has, *"stability only if the components are present all at the same time."* [13] L. K. Frank also raises some questions about the proper models to study organized complexities. He concludes that social scientists must be willing to relinquish old methods and replace them with new ones that are better suited to the study of complexity.[14]

The Conceptual Strategy Used

Keeping these problems in mind, how is one to proceed? The first task is to develop concepts that mirror reality accurately. Accurate coverage of reality does not necessarily mean a total coverage. It is the comprehension of all the *relevant* variables. Relevant variables are those that have causal effects.[15,16] To under-

---

[11] W. Ross Ashby, "General Systems Theory as a New Discipline," *General Systems,* Vol. III (1958), pp. 1–2.

[12] W. Ross Ashby, *Cybernitics* (London: Chapman and Hall, Ltd., 1958), p. 17.

[13] Gerard, *op. cit.,* p. 128. Italics are mine.

[14] L. K. Frank, "Research for What?" *Journal for Study of Social Issues,* Supplement, March, 1958.

[15] Kurt Lewin, *Field Theory in Social Science,* D. Cartwright (ed.) (New York: Harper & Bros., 1951), chap. 9.

[16] Ernst Cassirer, *Substance and Function and Einstein's Theory of Relativity* (Chicago: Open Court Publishing Co.), pp. 160 ff.

stand the cause of some phenomenon, one must be able to answer the questions, "What brings it about?" [17] The scientist must be able to describe the mechanisms which lead to the phenomena being studied [18] and relate these to the basic objectives of the system.

What are the relevant variables in studying organizations and how are they related to cause the phenomena under study? How is one to understand a pattern of variables whose interdependence is highly complex? These are extraordinarily difficult questions to answer. The variables are so numerous and the interrelationships so complex that one must be careful lest he miss the very complexity that is so characteristic of organizations.

One possibility is to assume that organizations, although complex in their present state, evolve from simple beginnings (let us say one or two variables) which once "fused" together, generated new variables, which in turn generated new ones, etc. This method of analysis is not unlike the one used by some scientists in trying to understand the beginnings of the universe. They begin by assuming the existence of a few variables. Knowing the properties of these variables, they can predict the output of their interaction. Once the output is understood new predictions can be made. The "evolutionary" thought process is continued until the present complexity is evolved. Another similar approach is that of the biologist who tries to understand growth. He is no longer satisfied with the idea that all the knowledge about growth lies within the cell. Many biologists are beginning to conceptualize their data in terms of "communities of cells" interacting with one another.

The same type of thinking may be valid for the study of social organization. For example, let us begin with the pattern of a social organization which, in essence, is a highly complex interrelationship of multilevel parts.

Each "part" is an activity with an intended consequence and resultant. As the resultants interact with one another, they lead to

---

[17] Hans Selye, *The Stress of Life* (New York: McGraw-Hill Book Co., Inc., 1956), p. 243.

[18] In the more advanced sciences the description is one conceptual level.

the development of more parts which have their own resultants which in turn interact to create new parts, etc. The birth of the new parts is not infinite. At some point (as yet unexplained) the "new" parts are adequate to achieve the objective to maintain the organization. Feedbacks develop to the "older" (previously born) but presently existing parts thereby creating a self-maintaining system with objectives, order, and boundaries.

One may summarize our position as follows. Theoretical explanations may be classified as genetic or dynamic. Genetic explanations are those which attempt to explain how an organism becomes what it is. Dynamic explanations focus on how the organism behaves at the present time.[19] Our strategy is to begin by developing a genetic model which, once completed will also provide dynamic explanations.

If we accept this strategy then the first step is to select a small number of variables with which to begin weaving the genetic theory. Formal organizations and human beings (both conceived as dynamic, goal-directed unities) may be chosen to be two basic variables. The next step is clear. What is known about the properties of each of these two unities? From this knowledge we should be able to predict the resultants when these two variables are "fused." [20] In this manner, we may be able (1) to enumerate the relevant variables, (2) to reconstruct the mechanisms by which they are created, and (3) to show how the parts are related to one another to create the whole.

A Theoretical Model of Organizational Behavior: A First Approximation

The writer has already attempted such a step. The results are reported in detail elsewhere. What follows *is only an outline.* By beginning with the research literature on the nature of personality and formal organization, he was able to evolve the beginnings of a theoretical framework which defines some of the relevant vari-

[19] Irving L. Janis, *et al, Personality and Persuasibility* (New Haven: Yale University Press, 1959), p. 22.

[20] At this point the approach is similar to that which E. W. Bakke discusses as the "fusion process." *The Fusion Process,* Labor and Management Center (New Haven: Yale University, 1953).

ables and their interrelationships (i.e., the processes by which they influence one another).

In order to provide the reader with an acquaintance of the framework, some of the basic propositions are outlined below. It must be emphasized again that what follows is a *summary outline* and much has been omitted in order to conserve space.[21]

The Development of the Individual in Our Culture

The development of the human personality can be hypothesized to follow the directions and dimensions outlined in the following model.

It is hypothesized that human beings in our culture:

a) Tend to develop from a state of passivity as infants to a state of increasing activity as adults. (This is what Erikson [22] has called self-initiative and Bronfenbrenner [23] has called self-determination.)

b) Tend to develop from a state of dependence upon others as infants to a state of relative independence as adults. Relative independence is the ability to "stand on one's own two feet" and simultaneously to acknowledge healthy dependencies.[24] It is characterized by the liberation of the individual from his childhood determiners of behavior (e.g., family) and developing his own set of behavioral determiners. This individual does not tend to react to others (e.g., the boss) in terms of patterns learned during childhood.[25]

c) Tend to develop from being capable of behaving only in a few ways as an infant to being capable of behaving in many different ways as an adult.[26]

---

[21] The interested reader is referred to Argyris, *op. cit.*

[22] E. H. Erikson, *Childhood and Society* (New York: W. W. Norton & Co., Inc., 1950). See also R. Kotinsky, *Personality in the Making* (New York: Harper & Bros.), pp. 8–25.

[23] Urie Bronfenbrenner, "Toward an Integrated Theory of Personality," in Robert R. Blake and Glen B. Ramsey, *Perception* (New York: Ronald Press Co., 1951), pp. 206–57.

[24] This is similar to Erikson's "sense of autonomy" and Bronfenbrenner's "state of creative interdependence."

[25] Robert W. White, *Lives in Progress* (New York: The Dryden Press, Inc., 1952), pp. 339 ff.

[26] Lewin and Kounin believe that, as the individual develops needs and abilities, the boundaries between them become more rigid. This explains why an adult is better able than a child to be frustrated in one activity and behave constructively in another. See Kurt Lewin, *A Dynamic Theory of Personality*

d) Tend to develop from having erratic, casual, shallow, quickly dropped interests as an infant to having deeper interests as an adult. The mature state is characterized by an endless series of challenges, where the reward comes from doing something for its own sake. The tendency is to analyze and study phenomena in their full-blown wholeness, complexity, and depth.[27]

e) Tend to develop from having a short time perspective (i.e., the present largely determines behavior) as an infant to a much longer time perspective as an adult (i.e., where the behavior is more affected by the past and the future).[28] Bakke cogently describes the importance of time perspective in the lives of workers and their families and the variety of foresight practices by means of which they seek to secure the future.[29]

f) Tend to develop from being in a subordinate position in the family and society as an infant to aspiring to occupy an equal and/or superordinate position relative to their peers.

g) Tend to develop from a lack of awareness of self as an infant to an awareness of and control over self as an adult. The adult who tends to experience adequate and successful control over his own behavior tends to develop a sense of integrity (Erikson) and feelings of self-work.[30] Bakke [31] shows that one of the most important needs of workers is to enlarge those areas of their lives in which their own decisions determine the outcome of their efforts.

A word about the concept of growth. Growth is not a black or white, mature or immature phenomenon. Rather it is a matter of degree. Thus each dimension is conceptualized to be a continuum upon which the development of any given human being can be plotted at a given time. In real life, the exact location of any given individual along the continua will differ and may also differ with

---

(New York: McGraw-Hill Book Co., Inc., 1935); and Jacob S. Kounin, "Intellectual Development and Rigidity," R. Barker, J. Kounin, and H. R. Wright (eds.), *Child Behavior and Development* (New York: McGraw-Hill Book Co., Inc., 1943), pp. 179–98.

[27] White, *op. cit.,* pp. 347 ff.

[28] Lewin also cites the billions of dollars that are invested in insurance policies. Kurt Lewin, "Time Perspective and Morale," in *Resolving Social Conflicts* (New York: Harper & Bros., 1948), pp. 105.

[29] E. W. Bakke, *The Unemployed Worker* (New Haven: Yale University Press, 1940).

[30] Carol R. Rogers, *Client-Centered Therapy* (Boston: Houghton Mifflin Co., 1952).

[31] E. W. Bakke, *op. cit.,* p. 247 and p. 29.

the same individual at different times. We do not assume that all individuals need to be or are at the right ends of the continua. We are presenting this as simply a model by which we can plot the individual differences of individual's growth pattern.

Keeping these qualifications in mind, we define *one* character-istic of a mature individual in *our* culture, as an individual who is predisposed toward the right ends (mature ends) of the con-tinua *and* who while striving towards growth behaves in such a way so that he *simultaneously permits others to do the same.* It is important to emphasize that our definition does not assume that a mature individual is a self-centered individual who is interested only in his own growth. Basic to our model is the assumption that all human beings are incomplete by themselves. They gain their wholeness through interaction with others. There is nothing new or startling about this position. We are simply following the ideas of men like Sullivan, Lewin, Fromm, McDougal, May, Rogers, Maslow, Rank, Horney, etc., that man is fundamentally an inter-personal organism. Self-actualization in the eyes of these scien-tists cannot occur in isolation. It can only occur in relationship with others. A mature individual therefore never assumes that he will be maximally independent, have complete control, and be completely active without inhibiting others' growth. To put it an-other way, one characteristic of a mature individual is hypothe-sized to be an individual who can give "of" himself without giv-ing "up" himself; an individual who sees himself as constantly being "in relationship" with his fellow man. "Self-actualization," as used here, does not mean "happiness," if by "happiness" we mean a relatively tensionless state where "everything is going my way." Tension per se may be quite healthy and provide motiva-tion for growth.[32]

Organization Is a Strategy

Next we turn to the organization and begin by hypothesizing that organizations are intricate human strategies designed to

[32] Gordon W. Allport, "The Trend in Motivational Theory," *American Journal of Ortho.*, Vol. XXIII, No. 1 (January, 1953), pp. 107–19. Roger Barker, Tamara Dembo, and Kurt Lewin found that a mild frustration could increase children's degree of contructiveness of play. *Frustration and Regression* (University of Iowa Studies in Child Welfare, 1941).

achieve certain objectives. What are the organization's objectives? The objectives are postulated to be achieving its goals (intended consequences), maintaining itself internally, and adapting to its external environment.

Who chooses the strategy that the organization will follow? In order to answer the question properly, the time dimension must be considered. *At the outset,* those who sign the legal charter to create the organization have much to say as to how it shall be organized. They plan an organizational structure which they assume represents the best strategy for the organization. Because of historical reasons too complex to discuss here, the basic characteristics of the structure are usually defined by generalizations from economics, scientific management, public administration, and traditional formal organization theory. This strategy is crystalized, "photographed," and represented as a typical organizational chart.

Let us look more closely at the nature of the phenomena depicted by the organizational chart.

The Intended Rationality of Formal Organization

The first requirement (or the first characteristic of the strategy) is for the organization to be rational and to make rational demands upon the employees. Thus the initial or formal structure represents the intended rational strategy of the organization. Urwick,[33] one of the pioneers in formal organizational theory describes the property of intended rationality eloquently. He insists that the creation of a formal organization requires a logical "drawing-office" approach. Although he admits that "nine times out of ten it is impossible to start with a clean sheet," the organizer should sit down and in a "cold-blooded, detached spirit . . . draw an ideal structure."

The task of the organizer, therefore, is to create a logically ordered world where Fayol suggests there is a "proper order" and in which there is a "place for everything (everyone)." [34]

---

[33] Urwick, *The Elements of Administration* (New York: Harper & Bros., 1953).

[34] Harold Koontz and Cyril O'Donnell, *Principles of Management* (New York: McGraw-Hill Book Co., Inc., 1955), p. 24.

The possibility that the formal organization can be altered by personalities, as found by McGregor and Arensberg [35] and Stodgill and Koehler,[36] is not denied by formal organizational experts. Urwick, for example, states that the planner must take into account the human element. But not that he perceives these adjustments as "temporary deviations from the pattern in order to deal with idiosyncrasy of personality." If possible, these deviations should be minimized by careful prior planning.

Some Basic Principles of Formal Organization [37]

Along with the emphasis upon rationality is the specialization of tasks, the emphasis upon power, conformity to and loyalty for company objectives. These emphases are embodied in four principles (more accurately assumptions) of scientific management theories.

Briefly these principles may be stated as follows:

1. Task (Work) Specialization. If concentrating effort on a limited field of endeavor increases the quality and quantity of output, organizational and administrative efficiency is increased by specialization of tasks assigned to the participants of the organization.

2. Chain of Command. The principle of task specialization creates a plurality of parts, each performing a highly specialized task. However, a plurality of parts busily performing their particular objective does not form an organization. A pattern of parts must be formed so that the interrelationships among the parts create the organization. Following the logic of specialization the planners create a new function (leadership) whose primary responsibility shall be the control, direction, and co-ordination of the interrelationships of the parts and to make certain that

---

[35] Conrad M. Arensberg and Douglas McGregor, "Determination of Morale in an Industrial Company," *Applied Anthropology,* Vol. I, chap. 2 (January–March, 1942), pp. 12–34.

[36] Ralph M. Stodgill and Kathleen Koehler, *Measures of Leadership Structure and Organization Change,* Personal Research Board (Columbus, Ohio: Ohio State, 1952).

[37] Some illustrative names are Urwick, Mooney, Holden *et al,* Fayol, Dennison, Brown, Gulick, White, Gauss, Steve Hopf, and Taylor. For a more detailed discussion see Argyris, *op. cit.,* chap. iii.

each part performs its objectives adequately. Thus the assumption is made that administrative and organizational efficiency is increased by arranging the parts in a determinate hierarchy of authority where the part on top can direct and control the part on the bottom.

If the parts being considered are individuals, then they must be motivated to accept direction, control, and co-ordination of their behavior. The leader is therefore assigned formal power to hire, discharge, reward, and penalize the individuals in order that their behavior be molded toward the organization's objectives.

3. Unity of Direction. If the tasks of every person in a unit are specialized, the objective or purpose of the unit must be specialized. The principle of unity of direction states that administrative and organizational efficiency increases if each unity has a single activity (or homogeneous set of activities) that is planned and directed by the leader.

4. Span of Control. The principle of control states that administration efficiency is increased by limiting the span of control of a leader to no more than five or six subordinates whose work interlocks.

The Impact of the Formal Organization upon the Individual [38]

What is the impact of the formal organization upon the individual? Clearly, the answer is that it depends upon the individual, the organization, and the context in which these are studied. Thus, as in our discussion of the human personality, we cannot state a priori what will happen in an individual case.

However, some position must be taken if generalizations are to be evolved. We must state the generalizations in such a way that when it comes time to use them in a particular organization, the uniqueness of the particular case will not be violated.

In developing our generalizations, therefore, we must assume a certain individual and a certain organization. *For the sake of illustration only* we will take as our example the case of a relatively mature individual and a formal organization that maxi-

---

[38] For a detailed discussion of these principles plus their impact upon the individuals see Argyris, *op. cit.,* chap. iii.

mizes the principles of scientific management (e.g., an organization with an assembly line). We select this case in order to make our point clearly and unambiguously and *not* because we want to imply that formal organizations are bad. On the contrary. In the example we have chosen we assume that the individual *and* the formal organization have a right to optimize their own expression.

The impact of the principles above is to place employees in work situations where (1) they are provided minimal control over their workaday world, (2) they are expected to be passive, dependent, and subordinate, (3) they are expected to have the frequent use of a few skin-surface shallow abilities, and (5) they are expected to produce under conditions leading to psychological failure.

All these characteristics are incongruent to the ones that relatively mature human beings in our culture are postulated to desire. They are much more congruent with the needs of infants in our culture. In effect, therefore, organizations adapt an initial strategy where they are willing to pay wages and provide adequate seniority if mature adults will, for eight hours a day, behave in a less than mature manner.

Stating the findings up to this point about the nature of organization in terms of propositions they are:

Proposition I: There Is a Lack of Congruency between the Needs of Healthy Individuals and the Demands of the (Initial) Formal Organization. If one uses the traditional formal principles of organization (i.e., traditional chain of command, task specialization, etc.) to create a social organization, and if one uses as input, agents who tend toward a mature state of psychological development (i.e., they are predisposed toward relative independence, activeness, use of their important abilities, control over their immediate work world) then a disturbance is created because the needs of healthy individuals listed above are not congruent with the requirements of formal organization, which tends to require the agents to work in situations where they are dependent, passive, use few and unimportant abilities, etc.

Corollary 1. The disturbance will vary in proportion to the degree of incongruency between the needs of the individuals and the requirements of the formal organization. An administrator is, therefore, always faced with an inherent tendency toward continual disturbance. Drawing on the existing knowledge of the human personality, a second proposition can be stated.

Proposition II: The Resultants of This Disturbance Are Frustration, Failure, Short Time Perspective, and Conflict. If the participants in the organization desire a healthy, more mature self-actualization:

1. They will tend to experience frustration because their self-expression will be blocked.
2. They will tend to experience failure because they will not be permitted to define their own goals in relation to central needs, the paths to these goals, etc.
3. They will tend to experience short time perspective because they have no control over the clarity and stability of their future.
4. They will tend to experience conflict because, as healthy agents, they will dislike frustration, failure, and short time perspective which is characteristic of the present job. However, if they leave they may not find a new job easily, and/or even if a new job is found, it may not be different.

Based upon the analysis of the nature of formal organization, one may state a third proposition.

Proposition III: Under Certain Conditions the Degree of Frustration, Failure, Short Time Perspective, and Conflict Will Tend to Increase. The resultants of the disturbance in the organization will tend to increase in degree:

1. As the individual agents increase in degree of maturity and/or
2. As the degree of dependence, subordination, passivity, etc., increases, this tends to occur:
    a) As one goes down the chain of command
    b) As directive leadership increases
    c) As management controls are increased
    d) As human relations programs are undertaken but improperly implemented and/or
3. As the jobs become more specialized, and/or

4. As the exactness with which the traditional formal principles are used increases.

Proposition IV: The Nature of the Formal Principles of Organization Cause the Subordinates, at Any Given Level, to Experience Competition, Rivalry, Intersubordinate Hostility and to Develop a Focus toward the Parts Rather than the Whole.

1. Because of the degree of dependence, subordination, etc., of the subordinates, upon the leader, and because the number of positions above any given level always tend to decrease, the subordinates aspiring to perform effectively [39] and to advance will tend to find themselves in competition with, and receiving hostility from each other.

2. Because according to the formal principles, the subordinates are directed towards and rewarded for, performing their own task well, the subordinates tend to develop an orientation toward their own particular part rather than towards the whole.

3. This part-orientation increases the need for the leader to co-ordinate the activity among the parts in order to maintain the whole. This need for the leader, in turn, increases the subordinates' degree of dependence, subordination, which creates a circular process whose impact is to maintain and/or increase the degree of dependence, subordination, etc., plus the rivalry and competition for the leader's favor.

Proposition V: Employees React to the Formal Organization by Creating Informal Activities. Continuing from Proposition II, it can be shown that under conflict, frustration, failure, and short time perspective, the employees will tend to maintain self-integration by creating specific adaptive (informal) behavior such as: [40]

1. Leaving the organization.
2. Climbing the organizational ladder.

---

[39] These problems may not arise for the subordinate who decides to become apathetic, disinterested, etc.

[40] Adaptive activities numbered one to nine become major categories under which much empirical research can be included.

3. Manifesting defense reactions such as daydreaming, aggression, ambivalence, regression, projection, etc.
4. Becoming apathetic and disinterested toward the organization, its make-up and goals. This leads to such phenomena as:
   a) Employees reduce the number and potency of the needs they expect to fulfill while at work.
   b) Employees goldbrick, set rates, restrict quotas, make errors, cheat, slow down, etc.
5. Creating informal groups to sanction the defense reactions and apathy, disinterest, and the lack of self-involvement.
6. Formalizing the informal groups.
7. Evolving group norms that perpetuate the behavior outlined in 3, 4, 5, and 6 above.
8. Evolving a psychological set that human or nonmaterial factors are becoming increasingly unimportant while material factors become increasingly important.
9. Acculturating the youth to accept the norms discussed in 7 and 8.

Comparing the informal organization, we may state:

Proposition VI: The Employee Adaptive Behavior Maintains Individual Self-Integration and Simultaneously Facilitates Integration with the Formal Organization.

Proposition VII: The Adaptive Behavior of the Employees Has a Cumulative Effect, Feeds Back into the Formal Organization, and Reinforces Itself.

1. All these adaptive reactions reinforce each other so that they not only have their individual impact on the system, but they also have a cumulative impact. Their total impact is to increase the degree of dependence, submissiveness, etc., and increase the resulting turnover, apathy, disinterest, etc. Thus a feedback process exists where the adaptive mechanisms become self-maintaining.
2. The continual existence of these adaptive mechanisms tend to make these norms or codes which, in turn, act to maintain the adaptive behavior and to make it the proper behavior for the system.

3. If the above is valid, then employees who may desire to behave differently from the norms will tend to feel deviant, different, not part of the work community (e.g., rate busters).

The individual and cumulative impact of the defense mechanisms is to influence the output-input ratio in such a way that a greater input (energy, money, machines) will be required to maintain a constant output.

Proposition VIII: Certain Management Reactions Tend to Increase the Antagonisms Underlying the Adaptive Behavior. Those managements that base their judgment on the logics of the formal organization will tend to dislike the employee adaptive behavior. It follows, therefore, for these managements that they should tend to take those "corrective" actions that are congruent with the logics of formal organization. These actions tend to be:

a) Increasing the degree of directive leadership.

b) Increasing the degree of management controls.

c) Increasing the number of pseudohuman relations programs.

The first two modes of reaction tend to compound, reinforce, and help to maintain the basic disturbance outlined in Proposition I. It follows, therefore, that the behavior included in Propositions IV, VI, and VII will also be reinforced. (This is the behavior management desires to change in the first place.) The third mode of reaction tends to increase the distance and mistrust between employee and management because it does not jibe with the realities of the system within which the employees work.

One must conclude that the management behavior described in Proposition VIII primarily acts to influence the output-input ratio so that a much greater input is required to obtain the same constant output, or that a disproportionately higher input will be necessary for a given increment of increased output.

A Clarifying Comment about the Propositions

A word about the propositions outlined above. It is possible for a physical scientist to make such predictions as, if one passes electricity through wire, heat will result. However, he cannot predict a priori *how much* heat will result. The amount of heat can be predicted only by ascertaining the values of such variables as the length and type of wire, the capacity of the battery, the milieu in which the experiment is conducted, etc.

The propositions presented above are on a similar level of generalization. They make such predictions as the dependence, submissiveness, etc., that people will experience will tend to be caused by the formal organization, directive leadership, and managerial controls (to list three major variables). They predict that the dependence and submissiveness will frustrate the people and place them in conflict *if* the people aspire toward the mature ends of the continua listed above. They predict further that the people will tend to react by creating informal activities (e.g., apathy, indifference, goldbricking, rate-setting, etc.). Nothing is said however about *how much* dependence, submissiveness; *how much* conflict, frustration; *how much* apathy, indifference, etc. This is a matter of empirical research. The value of the theoretical propositions is that they guide the researcher in his choice of relevant variables and the probable relationships among these variables.

For example, one can predict that the conflict, frustration, etc., will tend to be high when the formal organizational structure, the directive leadership, and the controls require (*a*) "maturity-directed" people to be directed toward infancy [41] and (*b*) "infancy directed" people to be directed toward maturity. One can predict, therefore, that absenteeism, turnover, apathy, etc., will be as high when "mature" people are frustrated by being required to be immature as when "immature" people are frustrated by being required to be mature. Furthermore, one can predict that the conflict, frustration, etc. will tend to be minimal when (*c*) "infancy-directed" employees are required to behave immaturely and (*d*) "maturity-directed" employees are required to behave maturely. [42]

---

[41] The "amount" of conflict, frustration, etc. must be empirically ascertained by measuring the "maturity-directiveness" of the employees and the degree to which the organization requires that they be "infancy-directed."

[42] Case (a) was chosen to be illustrated in *Personality and Organization* be-

who imply that the approach assumes that employees must be "happy" (whatever that means). Happiness should be the objective of management practice. Nothing could be further from the position of the writer. First, the writer is not attempting to tell any administrator what his objectives ought to be. The writer's aim is to try to understand the causes of human problems within organizations. True, he has chosen a theoretical framework that has as one of its basic concepts the development of the individual in our culture. But, *this concept was chosen because with it and the concept of formal organization the writer was able to integrate much of the behavioral science research within organizations of which he was aware.*

The fact that the concept of self-actualization turns out to be important is *not* because the writer wishes to require administrators to emphasize it. The concept is crucial *because it helps to create a scheme that integrates much of the existing research.* It is true, however, that if the administrator decides to use this scheme then self-actualization would be a crucial variable. However, it also follows from the discussion of the interaction of the individual and the organization above that organizational actualization is equally important. *Each needs the other.* The exact degree of this need varies with the problem and the situation.

Perhaps some examples may be helpful to suggest in what type of cases self-actualization may be crucial for organizational survival. Let us postulate that human beings manifest psychological (as well as physiological) energy of one form or another. This is a postulate many personality theorists accept because energy concepts are the pillars of most personality theories.[50] Psychological energy may be postulated to vary with the state of mind, to be indestructible, and to be unblockable.[51] If these properties of psychological energy are valid, then the administrator may not ignore individual self-actualization. If the individual's actualization is low, then the amount of psychological energy

---

[50] George Kelley provides a most interesting discussion of the difficulties of the motivational or "energy" approach. *The Psychology of Personal Constructs,* Vol. I (New York: W. W. Norton & Co., Inc., 1955).

[51] Jurgen Ruesch and Gregory Bateson, *Communication: The Social Matrix of Psychiatry* (New York: W. W. Norton & Co., Inc., 1952).

that he has available to produce will be less than if his self-actualization is higher. Another example, may be related to tension. If we may hypothesize that coping with tension (the source of which an individual reports is beyond his control) requires much energy in the form of maintaining defenses, then it follows that uncontrolled tension can draw upon the energy that an individual will tend to have available to be productive.

Turning to another example, if the vast field of perceptual psychological research is valid, we may hypothesize that what a person "sees" or is able to consider in his awareness is partially a function of his needs (Asch, Bruener, Postman, etc.). This means that decision making can be critically affected by the self-actualization of an individual.[51a] If the individual's "needs" at work are related to defense mechanisms, then he may tend to narrow his range of tolerance to new ideas so that threatening ideas will not arise. Still another example may be found in the work of Schutz and others. They show evidence that the individual personality plays an important role in the effective functioning of groups.[52] These results have important implications in terms of the impact of self-actualization on such activities as decision making, planning, etc.[53] In still another crucial area of interest for the administrator, Gardner Murphy points out in his classic and sweeping analysis of human potentialities, the individual's degree of creativity and productivity (intellectual and emotional) is highly influenced by his self-actualization.[54]

Summary

Let us summarize the main ideas of the discussions up to this point.

[51a] Herbert Holt and M. E. Salveson, "A Psychoanalytic Study of Management," Mgt. Report #10 (New Canaan, Conn.: Center for Advanced Management, 1959).

[52] William C. Schutz, *FIRO: A Theory of Interpersonal Relations* (New York: Rinehart & Co., Inc., 1958).

[53] Some interesting studies which make explicit the importance of self-actualization are reported by: John C. Flanagan, "Leadership Skills: Their Identification, Development and Evaluation," Paper presented at the ONR-LSU Symposium on Leadership and Interpersonal Behavior, March 3–5, 1959.

[54] Gardner Murphy, *Human Potentialities* (New York: Basic Books, Inc., 1958), see especially parts iii and iv.

1. Organizations are grand strategies individuals create to achieve objectives that require the effort of many. For historical reasons, most social organizations follow a particular initial or formal strategy whose roots may be found in military theory, industrial economics, scientific management, and public administration.

2. The strategy derived from these roots leads to a pyramid-shaped, formal organization defined by such principles as chain of command, unity of direction, span of control, and task specialization. If this formal strategy works as it is intended, then the analysis could end here. Unfortunately, the formal organizational strategy hits some snags—the primary one being the individual human being.

3. Mutual adaptations take place where the organization modifies the individual's personality and the individual, through the informal activities, modifies the formal organization. These modifications become part of the organization.

4. A total organization therefore is more than the formal organization. Conceptualizing it as a behavioral system we may conclude that an organization is a composite of four different but interrelated subsystems resulting in the following kinds of behavior:

   a) The behavior that results from the formal organizational demands.

   b) The behavior that results from the demands of the informal activities.

   c) The behavior that results from each individual's attempt to fulfill his idiosyncratic needs.

   d) The behavior that is a resultant of the unique patterning for each organization of the three levels above.

From the Model to the Specific Case

As this theoretical model develops two activities should become possible. First, hypotheses should be derived, which are then tested by empirical research. These results, in turn, will help to modify the theoretical model to make it a more valid mirror of reality. This activity represents the objective of developing generalizations relevant to all organizations of concern to us here. But, as students of social organizations, we also need to focus on diagnosing a *specific* organization and to understand fully its specific complexity and uniqueness.

Understanding the uniqueness and complexity of a case by the use of a theory is a sign of an extremely advanced science. It may or may not be completely achievable in the study of organizational behavior. The theoretical model being evolved by the writer (and presented above) is underdeveloped and primitive. The gap between the theory and understanding a particular case is therefore large indeed. The most that the model does is to provide the researcher with a list of probable relevant variables and their interrelationships.

To fill in the gap between theory and reality, the writer is evolving from his research experiences and from reading the literature a set of guideposts. They form a "working point of view" which provides him with a crude methodological map to advise him on certain crucial but gross decisions regarding the research strategy. With the conclusion of each research project and the reading of new literature the "working point of view" is modified. Hopefully as the results of the research add to the theory, the necessity for the guideposts may diminish.

At this stage of the development, however, the guideposts are crucial especially in defining the basic nature of the research objectives and methods, influencing the attitudes of the researcher in his everyday data gathering activities, and finally in the analysis and reporting of the results.

SOME GUIDEPOSTS IN DIAGNOSING ORGANIZATIONAL BEHAVIOR

Conceptual Guideposts

The first assumption is that the way organization has been, and continues to be described, in the traditional literature of scientific management, public administration, industrial engineering, and industrial economics is not complete. The assumption is inferred from the numerous studies and the countless everyday observations that an organization is something more than what is published in the policies and practices and represented on the formal organizational charts.

Further evidence for the assumption is the literature that exists on the basic nature of organization as seen by biologists, physicists, chemists, medical researchers, anthropologists, some economists, and general system theorists.[55] There is an increasing awareness that organization (or system) is a very basic property of life; if not life itself. Recently, a student of individual psychology suggested that a more fruitful approach to the study of *individuality* is through understanding the *organization* of their critical choices.[56] If one takes this literature seriously (and the writer does), then one arrives naturally at the assumption that the basic

---

[55] Examples of writings that have been most helpful to me are: Roberts Morley, *Bio Politics* (London, Dent); Robert Redfield (ed.), *Levels of Integration in Biological and Social Systems* (Lancaster: Jacques Cattel Press, 1942); James K. Feibleman, "Theory of Integrative Levels," *Brit. J. Phil. of Science,* Vol. V, and XVII (May, 1954), pp. 59–66; S. F. Nadel, *The Foundations of Social Anthropology* (London: Cohen and West, Ltd., 1951), pp. 29–30; Kenneth Boulding, *The Image* (Ann Arbor: Univ. of Michigan Press, 1956); M. J. Klein, "Order, Organization, and Entrophy," *Brit. J. Phil. of Science,* Vol. IV (1953); Thomas A. Szasz, "Entrophy, Organization and Problems of the Economy of Human Relationships," *Int. J. of Psychoanalyses,* Vol. XXXVI (July–Oct., 1955), pp. 289–97; "Profits and Problems of Homeostatic Models in the Behavioral Sciences; Chicago Behavioral Sciences, No. 1, Ludwig Von Bertalanffy and Anatol Rapoart (eds.), *General Systems,* Yearbook of the Society for the Advancement of General Systems Theory, Vol. I (1956); Ludwig Von Bertalanffy, *Problems of Life* (New York: John Wiley & Sons, Inc., 1952); Ludwig Von Bertalanffy, "Problems of General System Theory," *Human Biology,* Vol. XXIII, No. 4 (Dec., 1951), pp. 302–12; Edmund W. Sinnott, *Cell and Psyche* (University of North Carolina Press, 1950); *Biology and Teleology Bios.,* Vol. XXV, No. 1 (March, 1954); T. C. Schneirla, "The 'Levels' Concept"; John H. Rohrer and Muzafer Sherif, *Social Psychology at The Crossroads* (Harper & Bros., 1951), pp. 18–120; Kurt Goldstein, *The Organism* (New York: American Book Co., 1939); Henry Margenau, *The Nature of Physical Reality* (New York: McGraw-Hill Book Co., Inc., 1950); Tsune Shirai, "Systematic Models Social Groups," *Canad. J. Psychol.* (University of Toronto Press), Vol. VII, No. 8, pp. 126–32; Floyd H. Allport, *Theories of Perception and the Concept of Structure* (New York: John Wiley & Sons, 1955); A. Mace, "Homeostasis, Needs and Values," *Brit. J. Psychol.* (General Section), Vol. XXXX, Part 3 (August, 1953), pp. 200–210; Edmund W. Sinnott, "The Biology of Purpose," *Amer. J. Ortho-Psychiatry,* Vol. XXII, No. 3 (July, 1952), pp. 457–68; and Ewen Cameron, *General Psychotherapy* (New York: Grune & Stratton, 1950).

[56] Leona E. Tyler, "Toward a Workable Psychology of Individuality," *American Psychology,* 1959, pp. 75–81.

properties of human or social organizations are fundamentally similar to those organizations existing on different levels of analysis. Not only is this assumption an act of faith; it is a deep hope. If someday it can be integrated through the concept of organization then an important step will have been taken in unifying knowledge.[57]

The present objective of the writer in reading the literature is to help him formulate propositions about the nature of organization that cannot be found in the traditional formal organization. These propositions, it should be emphasized, do *not* form a theory. They are merely the beginnings of a framework that someday may evolve into a useful theory.

Some examples of propositions that the writer has evolved from his reading and uses as basic guideposts are: An organization is characterized by an *arrangement* of parts that form a unity or whole which feeds back to help maintain the parts;[58] A "part" of an organization is actually an "organic" part in that it exists by virtue of its position in the pattern that is the whole;[59] The whole, in turn may be differentiated from the parts along two dimensions. First the whole has a different boundary than any given part (or subset of parts).[60] Second, the functional unity of the whole displays properties only revealed in the actual process of full operation of the whole.[61]

These propositions lead the writer to form his own tentative conceptual definition of organization. An organization is

1. A plurality of parts
2. Maintaining themselves through their interrelatedness, and
3. Achieving specific objectives,

---

[57] For an interesting discussion, see Murphy, *op. cit.*, pp. 254–56.

[58] Norbert Weiner, *The Human Use of Human Beings* (Boston: Houghton Mifflin Co., 1950).

[59] Cylde Kluckhohn, "Anthropology," in James C. Newman (ed.), *What Is Science* (New York: Simon & Schuster, Inc., 1955), pp. 356–57.

[60] P. G. Herbst, "Situation Dynamics and the Theory of Behavior System," *Beh. Science,* Vol. III, No. 1 (Jan., 1957), pp. 13–29; and Herbert A. Simon, "Comments on the Theory of Organization," *Amer. Pol. Sci. Rev.,* Vol. XLVI, No. 4 (Dec., 1952), pp. 1130–39.

[61] Paul W. Kurtz, "Human Nature, Homeostasis and Value," *Phil. and Pheno. Res.,* Vol. XVII, No. 1 (Sept., 1956), pp. 36–55.

4. While accomplishing 2 and 3 adapt to the external environment, thereby

5. Maintaining their interrelated state of the parts.

Methodological Guidepost

The reader may wonder how such theoretical notions can be of help to a researcher in planning his research strategy. Actually a number of specific research actions are implied in these theoretical ideas.

Understanding the Parts and Their Interrelationship to One Another. The first implication is that the research strategy in addition to understanding the parts should focus on the *patterning* of all the relevant parts as well as the objective of the whole. If the properties and the output of the whole are only revealed in the full operation of the whole, then one must focus the research to "capture" the wholeness of the unity under study.[62] It is possible that a research strategy may fail [63] if it assumes a series of "part" studies may be eventually added together and will provide insight into the whole. The writer learned, after a series of failures, that the leadership behavior (one part of an organization) could not be separated, *by the subjects,* from such parts as the managerial controls and the organizational structure.[64] In short the part (leadership) could not be studied separately from the whole.

As a result of this guidepost, the writer has been induced to conduct his present research in an already existing organization because he has been unable to recreate an organization in its full richness within the laboratory setting. In the final analysis until

---

[62] John L. Kennedy, "A 'Transition-Model' Laboratory for Research on Cultural Change," *Human Organization,* Vol. XIV, No. 3 (Fall, 1955), pp. 16–18.

[63] Psychologists who know the history of "Structuralism" are intimately acquainted with the limitations of such logic. For an interesting discussion of similar problems in biological research see, J. Z. Young, "The Evolution of Organization Within the Nervous System," *Adv. of Sci.,* Vol. XIV, No. 54 (Sept., 1957), pp. 48–57. Also the symposium in *Concepts of Biology* cited previously is relevant.

[64] Chris Argyris, "Organizational Leadership," O.N.R., Conference on Leadership and Interpersonal Behavior, L. Petrullo and Bernard Bass (eds.) (Louisiana State University, March, 1959).

the organizational researcher is able to create organizations as he desires and to control parts of them while he varies others, scientific progress will be inhibited.

Self-Maintenance Activities Are Important. The conceptual definition emphasizes the organization's tendency toward stability or constancy. This implies that research should focus on the specific mechanisms by which the parts create the whole and how the whole feeds back to maintain the parts. Change in an organization may not therefore be understood unless the "steady state" of the organization is first understood.[65] If this guidepost is valid then researchers need not enter arguments as to the importance of the study of change versus the tendency toward constancy. Both are important but the latter precedes the former.

The Research Will Tend to Be Multilevel in Scope. The "parts" of an organization exist on many levels. For example, there are individuals, informal groups (large and small), departments, divisions, cultural norms, etc. Since all the parts that are relevant need to be studied, the diagnostic methodology should cope with variables on different levels of analyses. It should be able to relate functionally personality, informal group, and formal organization variables (for example) without much difficulty. To relate functionally the variables to one another is to arrange them in a meaningful pattern and to be able to show the processes (mechanisms) that maintain this pattern. For example, one might have to construct a pattern where personality variables are related to informal group variables and those in turn to formal organization variables and the latter to cultural variables, etc. In short, the diagnostic methodology should take its cue from the nature of the phenomena under study and not from the traditional academic boundaries.

The Quantification of Variables Is Desirable. The diagnostic methodology should always be planned with the thought of the eventual quantification of all variables. Mathematics is one of the most precise and general languages available to man. The objectives of research are to make the diagnostic methods publicly

---

[65] Selye, *op. cit.*

verifiable and easily repeatable. Quantification is necessary if these objectives are to be achieved.

In aspiring to objectivity and quantification one must be cautious. In the early development of a field of study qualitative insights may bear much fruit.[66] For example, Robert Oppenheimer makes a plea for the naturalistic methods and the use of qualitative description in research and cautions against too early mathematization.[67] In this connection, one wonders about the relevance of Von Neumann's recent findings that the human mind may be understood by a mathematics *less* accurate than those presently required for available computers. Apparently the mind's ability to operate efficiently with a *less* accurate calculus gives it its distinctive human quality.[68]

The Desire to Understand.[69]   A basic motivation a scientist has toward his work is the desire to understand (and as a result predict and control) the phenomena upon which he is focusing. He is interested first in knowledge (awareness of the order of his universe). The practitioner may question this motive and desire that the researcher be more practical. However, the history of science is full of examples from which one may safely say the most practical and useful knowledge has come from research whose primary aim has been the addition to knowledge. In fact, the position taken here is that much pure research may not be possible unless the subjects view it as being useful for them. However, the attempt to make research meaningful does not necessarily imply that the researcher modify his methods to satisfy some immediate short-run objective. It is his task to show the importance of conducting basic studies. Once accepted, it behooves him to conduct the research in a way that minimizes the subject's defensiveness. In other words, the best guarantee the practitioner

---

[66] Melville Dalton, *Men Who Manage* (New York: John Wiley & Sons, Inc., 1959), chap. xi.

[67] Robert Oppenheimer, "Analogy in Science," *American Psychologist,* Vol. II, No. 3 (March, 1956), p. 135.

[68] John Von Neumann, *The Computer and the Brain* (New Haven: Yale University Press, 1958).

[69] I am assuming that it is not necessary to emphasize the importance of theory being flexible and, at the same time, aspiring for the simplest explanation possible.

has for the development of useful knowledge is to permit the scientist to conduct research whose objectives are primarily those of the "scientific game." As Cohen writes, "social science can thus in the long run best attain its goal only when those who cultivate it care more for the scientific game itself and for the meticulous adherence to its rule of evidence than for any of the uses to which their discoveries can be put." [70]

This is not to deny the importance of helping to improve the lot of mankind. It is simply to say that those who are actively engaged in improving human life draw heavily on the research pursued regardless of practical application. [71]

Guideposts Related to Establishing Effective Research Relationships

In the section below I should like to discuss some guideposts that I have found useful in establishing effective research relationships. I do *not* imply that all research in organizational behavior should be guided by these suggestions. The research relationships should be guided by the research strategy and the phenomena studied. I do believe that these guideposts are valid in the study of organized complexity and such variables as frustration, conflict, needs, abilities, level of aspiration, attitudes, values, etc.

The Research Relationship as a "Helping Relationship." Recently, Rogers has described quite effectively in another context the basic characteristics of an effective research relationship. Rogers speaks of establishing "helping relationships" when counseling people. The writer believes the same ideas are valid for a researcher-subject relationship. The researcher strives to be perceived by the subject as trustworthy and dependable. Rogers [72] states:

---

[70] Cohen, *op. cit.,* p. 374.

[71] D. W. Bronk, "Science and Humanity," *Science,* Vol. CIX, No. 7837 (May 13, 1949), p. 477.

[72] Carl R. Rogers, *The Characteristics of a Helping Relationship* (Madison: University of Wisconsin, Department of Psychology and Psychiatry, n.d.) pp. 11 ff.

I have come to recognize that being trustworthy does not demand that I be rigidly consistent, but that I be dependably real. The term congruent is one I have used to describe the way I would like to be. By this I mean that whatever feeling or attitude I am experiencing would be matched by my awareness of that attitude. When this is true then I am an unified or integrated person in that moment, and hence I can *be* whatever I deeply *am*. This is a reality which I find others experience as dependable.

Behaving in a congruent manner is by no means a simple task. It requires that the researcher communicate unambiguously who he is. It requires that the researcher respect his own feelings and needs as well as those of the subject. Also it requires that the researcher enter fully into the world of feelings and personal meanings of the subject and to be acceptant of these feelings. In essence, a research relationship is a deeply human, personal one in which the researcher and the subject should find deep satisfactions. Unless such a relationship is created the subjects' willingness to tell what they really know and to dig for information that is difficult to unearth, will be greatly decreased. Without this personal dimension in the research relationship the subjects are likely to resist the researcher either by open defiance or, more likely, through careful defenses.[73]

The Meaning of Objectivity.   One may hypothesize that objectivity in field studies may not necessarily mean the separation of the researcher from the subjects. A researcher may not be able to obtain much of the data he needs to study organization behavior if he attempts to remain "neutral," "pure," and "detached." If he is human, this will lead to a feeling of being alienated. If he is not, he will be unable to obtain the data he requires. In any case "his subjects" may feel alienated by his "objective" techniques which they feel show disrespect for their human qualities and which miss the complexity of the world he is studying; one of the most important attributes of organization.

The researcher, in studying organization behavior, may have to commit himself to the study of "molar" behavior; deeply per-

[73] For a discussion of the problems a researcher faces, see Chris Argyris, "Diagnosing Defenses against the Outsider," *Journal of Social Issues*, Vol. VIII, No. 3.

sonal behavior; behavior which can best be observed or reported by the subjects when they are acting naturally as "whole" human beings.

These requirements make it difficult for a researcher to seriously consider himself an objective instrument in the sense that what he observes or "measures" is completely independent of himself as a personality and of the role he is perceived as fulfilling as a researcher.[74] Some "tough-minded" physical scientists report similar conclusions about the difficulty of the separation of the researcher from his instruments.[75] One way for the researcher to become "objective" is to become as fully aware as is possible of his subjectivity and "measure" the impact his subjectivity is having upon the situation he is studying.[76]

The Subject's "Set" toward the Researcher Influences the Data He Will Provide. The researcher should recognize that the subjects are organisms with needs, goals, values, etc. They will have feelings about the researcher and his role. For example, it is understandable that an individual may feel hostile toward a researcher who asks him to expose his personal feelings, many of which the subject may not have been consciously aware. The subject may resent the apparent control the researcher seems to have (he asks all the questions) and the implied assumption that the researcher can understand the organization better than the participant. Moreover the subject may fear that the researcher will unearth and/or handle incorrectly data that are potentially threatening to him (as a subject).

The Researcher's Needs Influence the Research Relationships He Desires to Create.[77] The researcher needs to recognize that

[74] Rollo May; Ernest Angel; and Henri F. Ellenberger, *Existence* (New York: Basic Books, Inc., 1958), chap. ii.

[75] P. W. Bridgman, "Remarks on Niels Bohr's Talk," *Daedalus,* Spring, 1958, p. 175.

[76] Rollo May, "Historical and Philosophical Presuppositions for Understanding Therapy," in O. H. Mawrer, *Psychotherapy: Theory and Research* (New York: Ronald Press Co., 1953).

[77] Warren Bennis in an insightful paper discusses some of the impact of the researcher's and the therapist's needs in the conduct of group therapy research. See "Reflections on Some Problems Encountered in the Conduct of Group Therapy Research," Paper read at American Group Psychology Association, Annual Meeting, January, 1959, New York City.

he too is an organism with needs, which greatly influence his research. For example, the researcher's ideal of the creation of a highly structured research world, where the researcher can control and have power over people (especially undergraduates!) in order to experiment with them, may imply important needs motivating a researcher. The need to be needed, to have his intellectual powers publicly acclaimed may also be important. One can imagine the tension a researcher will tend to cause in an organization if he is defensive about his needs to control and dominate individuals. The subjects who feel this defensiveness may react negatively. A defensive researcher will tend to react in a hostile nonunderstanding manner. This, in turn, may tend to make the subject even more defensive, and we have completed a circular process leading to increased tension between the subject and the researcher. Under these conditions the subject will be poorly motivated to examine and report his personal views. Similarly, the researcher once under tension may unconsciously distort his observations of the subject and his subsequent analyses.[78]

The Researcher Aspires toward "Conscious Living." In the writer's experience it is important for the researcher to feel free to express himself as fully as possible in order that, by his behavior, he can communicate to the subject the feeling that he, too (the subject), might find it helpful to express himself unambiguously. The essence of research is to make life public and conscious. A researcher should live consciously for whatever is conscious may be understood and controlled. As Collier [79] points out, what one can talk about indicates what one can begin to manage.

Feedback as a Way to Increase Meaningfulness of Research to the Subjects. An equally crucial requirement is to make research

---

[78] In an interesting study it has been shown that the individual's ability to report a given social event accurately decreases as the person's images of himself are incongruent with the character of the event he is describing. Isthiel de Sola Pool and Irwin Shulman, "Newsmen's Fantasies, Audiences, and Newswriting," *Public Opinion Quarterly,* Summer, 1959, pp. 145–58.

[79] Rex M. Collier, "Consciousness as a Regulatory Field: A Theory of Psychotherapy," *Journal of Abnormal and Social Psychology,* Vol. LV, No. 3 (November, 1957), pp. 275–82; and Rex M. Collier, "Consciousness as a Regulatory Field: A Theory of Psychotherapy," *Psychological Review,* Vol. LXIII, No. 6 (1959), pp. 360–69.

meaningful to, and need-fulfilling for, the participants as well as to the researcher. The overwhelming evidence from personality, perception, child psychology, and psychotherapy is that an individual provides information most accurately when "information giving" is, for him, need fulfilling and nonthreatening.

One possible way to help make research a meaningful process for the subject is to include within its design areas of deep interest to the subjects.

How does one know what is of deep interest to the subject? The researcher may find it valuable to communicate to the subjects during the preliminary discussions that one of the problems they must work through is for them to develop a list of their major interests so that, wherever possible, they could be incorporated in the research design. The ensuing sessions can provide the researcher with an excellent opportunity to "expose" himself to the subjects and vice versa.

It is during these early discussions that the researcher can obtain valuable insight into (1) the degree of awareness various members of the organization have of their problems, (2) the degree of agreement among the various diagnoses, (3) the degree of defensiveness of different individuals, and (4) the probable reaction of the individuals to the research results.

The last information is very important. In the writer's opinion one of the most difficult problems is a highly motivated management who wants to support research but who in the researcher's opinion would not tend to deal with the feedback information constructively. For example, in one situation the executives inferred from the feedback that the management ought to behave in a way so that the subordinates' dependence, submissiveness, etc., be reduced. The president was enthusiastic. He pounded the table and said to the top executives, "All right, our goal is clear. We've got to sell democratic leadership. We've got to be enthusiastic and sell this goddam stuff whenever we can. I am sure it will work."

Another way to involve the subject in the research is through feedback of the information obtained.

Some researchers feed back information periodically to the

subjects. The frequency may vary from one at the end [80] to periodically,[81] to daily.[82] In the writer's experience feeding back information may alter significantly the "whole" he is studying. This would violate the first working principle. Consequently, whenever requests are made for feedback, the writer first accepts the requests and thanks the subjects for their interest. The researcher than admits that he would enjoy feeding back information especially if it may be helpful to the subjects. However, he points out something that was discussed at the outset and placed in a letter of agreement; namely, that in order to fulfill his research needs *and* be most helpful to the organization he ought to understand it thoroughly before feedback is attempted. If the suggestion is rejected, the researcher may have to terminate the study.

Feedback Can Be Threatening to Subjects and to the Researcher. If the researcher's suggestion to study the organization carefully before he issues a diagnosis is accepted, his difficulties have just begun. Conducting research in an organization tends to make the researcher a fountain of knowledge about the organization. In many instances he discovers data that contradict and/or go beyond the views held by management or the employees. The feedback of results therefore tends to be a potentially disturbing situation to the participants—especially to those in power. This would be true of the researcher if his organization is studied. It is not easy for them to accept emotionally the possibility that they do not know their own organization as well as does an outsider (a researcher at that)! It also implies that the researcher may be more competent than the subject in coping with human relationships. Finally, the administrators may feel that the employees, by communicating information to the researcher that is new to them have bypassed them or implied that they lack the freedom

[80] Rensis Likert, and Floyd Mann, "The Need for Research on Communication Research Results," *Human Organization*, Vol. XI (Winter, 1952), pp. 15–19; and Floyd Mann, "Studying and Creating Change," in C. Arensberg (ed.), *et al, Research in Industrial Human Relations* (New York: Harper & Bros., 1957), pp. 146–70.

[81] Personal communication with Professor W. F. Whyte.

[82] Elliot Jaques, *The Changing Culture of a Factory* (London: Tavistock Publications, 1951).

necessary to communicate to management some of their personal feelings.

Not only is the act of feedback potentially threatening, but the executives may view it as being a hostile act. First, the researcher may embarrass the administration by communicating to them, as a group, information which they never discuss as a group. Second, the administrators may feel hostile to the researcher for withholding information that he could have fed back months ago. It is not too difficult for already defensive administrators to conclude that the researcher purposely withheld the information till the feedback meeting to embarrass the management and/or to psychologically "clobber" them.

Feedback May Provide Basis for Effective Relationships. Although the feedback situation is potentially explosive it also has the potentiality of laying the foundation for a truly effective researcher-subject relationship. The researcher can use the feedback situation to show by his own behavior that he is neither threatened by, nor reacts defensively against, a group that feels it must be hostile toward him. If he can, through actual behavior, communicate to the members that they may be quite hostile to him (when they feel they must) he has helped to establish a sounder researcher-subject relationship. In the writer's experience no matter how much hostility is generated during feedback the final evaluation of him (by the group) is made in terms of how well he understood and accepted their feelings and not so much whether his views are in agreement with the management.

The above does not mean to imply that much of the fine work done with the use of objective questionnaire approach in invalid. Many valuable studies have been conducted and many valuable insights and generalizations have been evolved when the questionnaire is in the hands of a competent researcher. However, it is the position of the writer that questionnaires may be used most effectively during the early stages of research. As the researcher desires to dig deeper and to study such phenomena as frustration, apathy, alienation, hostility, blocking, rationalizations, etc., he will have to create a more "human" research relationship where the respondent is in a face to face relationship with the researcher.

Wiedorn provides some interesting insights into the problem when he analyzes the conditions that need to be met if a *researcher* is to study psychiatric problems. He states: [83]

1. Data pertaining to these processes exists experimentally or observationally only in an interpersonal relationship (with real or fantasied other persons). The extent to which mechanical recording devices may reproduce and allow experiencing of such processes is little known and is an area needing much investigation.
2. These data may be communicated to an observer only through and within an interpersonal relationship.
3. Communication to the observer necessitates the observer being or becoming a participant in the interpersonal relationship.
4. Upon the observer becoming a participant in the experimental interpersonal relationship, both observer and observed persons become part of the interpersonal relationship. Both parties contribute to and share in the process under observation. In such a situation distance between the observed person and the observer decreases and in a sense, becomes nil.
5. The observer, as well as being a participant in the process studied, is simultaneously the instrument of observation and recording, and organizing of the data so gathered.

These then are some of the basic assumptions that are used in guiding the researcher in his selection, conceptualization, and study of problems. The next step is to see how the theoretical framework and the guideposts are used to help the researcher select the research instruments, define the questions, and analyze the data that he obtains.

---

[83] William S. Wiedorn, Jr., "Method in Research in Psychiatry: Implications for the Philosophy of Science," *Philosophy of Science,* Vol. XXV, No. 4 (October, 1958), p. 260.

CHAPTER

II

Diagnostic Procedures

HAVING DISCUSSED the theory and methodology, we now turn to the actual research methods and instruments used. The writer is experimenting with many different types of methodological tools including nonparticipant, participant-observation, and the semi-structured research interview. Each has its advantages and disadvantages. The choice therefore depends upon the problem being studied, the type of "research permission" granted, the relationship established with the subjects, the time available, and the state of development of the research methods.

For the particular types of problems studied and the models reported in this book, the semistructured interview seems to provide the maximum return on research investment. Consequently, it is the one that can be reported in some detail at this time. It is expected that the development of the other methods will be reported in detail in future publications.

The Semistructured Research Interview

The semistructured research interview seems especially suited for the lower-level employees whose (immediately evident) behavior is highly controlled by the technology. In the writer's experience most of the employees' spontaneous behavior related to their human problems tends to exist on a thought, feeling, and even dream level and therefore cannot be tapped easily either by asking direct questions or by observing them.

In the interview, questions can be asked which permit the employees to project their more unconscious thoughts and to share those views about which they may be more defensive. For example, the question, "If you were hiring someone for a job like yours, what kind of person would you look for?" can provide rich material about the respondent's personal inner tensions and the difficulties which he relates to the organization.

The interview, however, has some serious limitations. The strongest limitation is related to the gap between how people say they behave and how they actually behave. This gap is especially crucial when studying the upper levels of management. In the long run it may turn out that upper management must be studied primarily by observational methods. An example of the difficulties involved is related to the observation that many top executives are quite defensive about the power they hold. They like to believe in the cultural (political) ideal of democratic leadership and tend to view themselves as leading "equals" in a "down-to-earth manner." Below is an illustration of the discrepancy between what a manager says in an interview about his relationships with the subordinates and how he actually behaves.

During the interview the manager makes such comments as:

Well, I think the most important thing is co-operation between supervision and employees. There should be a feeling of friendship. You shouldn't look down on the worker. I treat people as if we're all on the same level. It seems to me that's the human way.

Over-all relations are very cordial, extremely cordial, because most of us have worked our way up. That's a wonderful thing about this company, and I think because I've had to work my way up, I realize the problems a worker has.

Human relations between the supervisors and the employees is not only crucial, but it's becoming more crucial. It's more important now than it was in the past. And it takes a long time to get the skill, a long time. Now, not that I want to set myself up as an expert, but it took me a long time. Many problems that you could have, could have been averted if these men had better training.

Now let us turn to a segment of an observation made of the same manager leading a meeting with the foremen.

MANAGER: Now, fellows I want you to know that we're not up to our production schedules. We're not up to the production schedules that you yourselves set up a couple of months ago. Now let me show you the figures. For example, you guys are 100 dozen behind. Can you imagine that? 100 dozen. Then take over here, in the supply room. Why we're averaging—you told us you were going to average 90 gross a day, you're only averaging 62. Now these kinds of figures really bother me, fellows, and there's something that has to be done about it, damn it. Something has to be done.

It seems to me that you fellows are nowheres near the schedules that you set up at the beginning of the year. Now something's wrong.

FOREMAN A: Well, I think this month is going to be a little better. You got this month's results?

MANAGER: Well, this includes just right to February and that doesn't look too good.

FOREMAN B. (Tries to tell Foreman A his figures are pretty good.)

MANAGER: I disagree with you now. I'd say you're wrong. Just a minute I'll show you. (Foreman A takes out a book which is full of figures, and points to them.) Now look at this, just take a look at those figures—now that doesn't compare with what you said. I don't think there's any excuse for this drop, gentlemen, and we've got to do something about it. We've got to build this up and build it up fast, that's all there is to it. For example, let me show you what the hell the departments are doing. Department A is in the red $5,000; Department B is in the red $2,000. You know we're operating on extra work at a loss of $968. This is very bad, it seems to me.

Christ, take a look at this, terrible. Now how the hell do we make a product shaped like this, can you tell me? I've been in this business 30 years and this is the first time I've seen such a thing.

Although the discrepancy between how the manager behaves and how he says he behaves is large, a skilled interviewer during the interview could ask appropriate questions from which he could infer how valid the manager's description is of himself. For example, immediately after the manager gave the first quotation, the interviewer said, "This is most interesting. Would you please help me to understand it better. How does a manager create feelings of friendship?" The manager replied, "Well, that's simple, I told you, I treat individuals as human beings." The researcher counters, "Yes, this is precisely what I am trying to understand. It is difficult for me to visualize the actual behavior of a manager when he is treating people as human beings. Could you help me perhaps by giving an example?" Such a line of questioning may be continued until the researcher is able to assess the degree to which the manager describes his actual behavior accurately. If a discrepancy exists, it may be immediately flagged by the researcher and nonparticipant observations which are then scheduled to observe how the manager does behave.

It is action such as this that helps the researcher to overcome some of the serious limitations of the interview approach thereby permitting him to use it as the key research method.

The Research Strategy Underlying the Questions Asked during the Interview

Before the questions used during the interview are described, the research strategy that underlies their selection should be presented.

1. The questions should be so worded and organized that they can result in an interpersonal research relationship that permits the researcher and the subject to feel at ease and to be as spontaneous as each desires.

2. The questions should serve as stimuli for the respondent to discuss certain *areas* of activities and feelings. "Yes" or "no" questions should be minimized. If respondents do answer in one or two words, the interviewer should prod further to better understand what reasons lie behind the short answers. If possible, examples should be obtained. If the respondent's answer is a lengthy one, the interviewer should "feed back" his perception of the answer to the respondent for a "validity check." For example, "If I understand you correctly, you feel . . . ?"

3. Although the questions are pretested, the interviewer should not assume that the "pretested" meaning of the questions is the meaning which the respondent will perceive. Some factors that can "cause" the respondent to "hear" the question in a different way are psychological limitations, status position in the organization, feelings related to organization, the self-concept of the individual, the potential threat of the interviewer, and interview situations. It is not important for the interviewer to put the ques-

tion in exactly the same way to all the respondents. It *is* important to ask the question in such a way that the interviewer can infer that the respondent will tend to understand the question in the manner in which the interviewer intends. The exact statement of the question, therefore, may vary as the interviewer infers certain personality and/or organizational and/or situational factors that may be operating to impede clear and direct transmission and reception of messages.

4. Once the respondent begins to discuss the area, the interviewer feels free to ask whatever further questions he deems necessary to explore the full dimension of the questions. Some respondents will "tell you everything" with one question. Others need further questioning to elicit from them all the necessary information.

The questions, therefore, are viewed as "tools" with which to explore "unknown territory." The interviewer should feel free to utilize as many "tools" as he feels are necessary.

5. The interview begins with somewhat "objective" and assumed (by the researcher) less threatening questions. The interviewer need not maintain the exact order of questioning that is on the "work sheet." The most fruitful and "research-insightful" order is the one the respondent chooses.

To summarize, the success of the interview is largely dependent upon the interviewer. Some of the most important abilities that he requires are asking questions in such a way that neither he nor the respondent becomes defensive, clarifying thoughts without implying solutions, and restating accurately the respondent's contribution in order to check that he has been understood and to provide the respondent with an opportunity to expand or modify.

But skilled interviewing is not enough. Another important requirement is that the interviewer be aware of the relevant research so that he can take full advantage of what he hears. If the respondent makes a statement from which the researcher infers that the employee feels tension due to frustration, then he must check this inference before the interview is over. A thorough knowledge of the concept of frustration is vital if he is going to ask the "right questions." Helping the respondent to spell out his feelings may lead the interviewer to conclude whether or not he is correct. Since the raw data from which he makes his inference are always included (the interviewer writes during the interview), independent checks are made of his inferences. (Some of these checks are discussed in Chapter III.)

When an interviewer deals with factors like frustration, tension, conflict, aggression, and other defenses of the human personality, he is working in a very difficult area. Even with the most "objective" definitions of these factors, there is still a strong possibility that the interviewer can become defensive and attribute to the respondent feelings and needs that are really his. For example, the writer knows that as a result of studies of his interviewing, he tends to "see" more aggression in situations than do other observers. He may decide that he wants to know why he does this (which he did decide) but this is not mandatory. If the people making the analysis know of his biases, they can account for them when they are analyzing the data that he obtains. In short it is crucial that the interviewer be aware of his own self-concept and its impact upon his research activities.

The Questions Used and Their Research Objectives

The kind of questions asked and the areas tapped are related to the theoretical framework and the guideposts. Every question has a primary objective which is to obtain information needed about a specific dimension inferred from the theory. Each question also has two secondary objectives. The first is to act as an internal consistency or validity check for one or more questions. A validity check is the comparison of one answer to a question with the answer to another designed to get at the same or related information but worded differently.

If the content of a question appears to conflict with the answers given to related questions, the question is carefully scrutinized. If the conflict is related to idiosyncratic behavior or personality level of analyses, it is simply eliminated if it cannot be reconciled. If the conflict is related to group or organizational activities, it is then checked with other interviews. Examples are given below of some possible validity checks for the first five questions.[1] A detailed presentation is found in Figure 1, page 52.

The other secondary objective is to add and deepen the information available about other related areas. Perhaps the best way to clarify the procedure is to cite some examples. All the questions on the interview schedule are presented below along with an indication of their primary and secondary functions.

Question 1: Let us begin with what do you do? What is the title of your job? Would you help me to get to know your work better by describing a typical day? Perhaps you might like to begin with what you feel are your most imporant activities?

This is a warm-up question assumed to be nonthreatening. Assumption found to be false when respondent feels he has a degrading, ambiguous, undesirable, or inaccurate title.

Added Information: Provides insight into requirements of jobs and initial attitudes toward jobs. Respondents obtaining adequate satisfactions tend to speak enthusiastically and at length about their work. They tend to emphasize the job's interrelationships. Respondents not gaining self-expression tend to give short, primitive, cursory answers.

Question 2: How would you describe your job: Would you say it is routine, monotonous or different and full of variety (vary these two choices systematically)?

On the basis of experience it seems that a natural follow-up is to ask how the respondent views his job now that he has described it. This paves the way to discuss satisfactions.

Added Information: Begins to provide information as to the kinds of demands the job makes of the individual. Respondents rarely limit themselves to discussing simply the routine-variety dimensions. Also provides information regarding satisfactions or at least paves the way for the discussion of satisfactions.

Question 3: What sorts of personal satisfactions if any can a person obtain from a job like yours?

Respondents (especially those who feel that for years they have worked on nonchallenging jobs) tend to have difficulty

---

[1] The word "possible" is used to represent the theoretically known possibilities. The actual depends upon what information a given respondent provides.

with the phrase "personal satisfactions." The difficulty itself becomes added data to the researcher and provides an excellent point of departure.

Added Information: May provide added information about the nature of the job, relationship with the management and with other employees. May provide information regarding personal needs and aspirations.

Question 4: How much freedom would you say you have on the job? By that I mean how much leeway do you feel you have to do the job the way you desire?

Added Information: Possible information on the respondents' need to be dependent, independent, etc. Possible impact of formal organizational policies and practices, controls, and leadership patterns.

Question 5: If you were hiring someone for a job similar to yours, what sort of a person would you look for? For example, what abilities do you think he should have?

Added Information: Pressure respondent feels on job. Respondent's views of the demands made on others.

Question 6: If you were hiring a foreman for a department like yours what kind of a foreman would you hire? How do you feel a good foreman behaves?

Added Information: Insight on foremen leadership patterns. Insight on pressures brought by the technology, controls and policies. Insight on respondent's dependency needs.

Question 7: How do you think the employees in your department feel about the kitty? How important would you say is the kitty?

This question deals with one of the company's control schemes, namely the incentive pay. Employees who may do exceptionally well one day may set aside some money in their personal "kitty" for a day when the jobs might be so difficult that it becomes impossible to achieve a fair day's pay. (Discussed in detail in the next chapter.)

Added Information: Added information on the degree of freedom an employee has on the job. Infer about leadership in terms of its actions toward the kitty since it is officially illegal. Infer personality aspects of respondent in terms of his desire to control his own world.

Question 8: In answering the next question please free free not to limit yourself to your job. Let us focus on you as an individual. What would you say are your important abilities? What are the things you feel you can do well?

Added Information: Provides important insights into needs, aspirations, and values of the respondent. Provides insight into the potency of the work situation. Can the respondent "forget it" for the moment. Provides insight into the degree to which his job provides possibilities for self-expression.

Question 9: How often would you say you come in contact with your boss during a typical day? What sort of things do you talk about?

Added Information: Insights into respondent's relationship with his boss. Subjective quantification such as "not enough" or "too much" provide points of exploration of rich data. Insight into dependency needs.

Question 10: How do you feel about the trips the top brass make throughout the plant stopping and saying hello to people?

Added Information: Provides information regarding dependency needs of employees. Provides information on impact of leadership patterns of top management.

Question 11: How do you think others feel about the wages? Are there any other rewards one can look for in this plant?

Added Information: Insight into the views about the piece-rate system and other managerial controls. Insight into views regarding job security and benefits.

Question 12: Let us think back to the first day that you came to work. What made you pick X Company? How did you decide to choose this plant?

Added Information: Summation of these answers may provide a picture of how organization is viewed by the outside environment. Bakke calls this the "organization's charter." [2] Insight into respondent's personality especially his level of aspiration and

---

[2] E. W. Bakke, *The Fusion Process,* Labor and Management Center (New Haven: Yale University Press, 1954).

goals. Insight into factors employees consider in making job choices.

Question 13: Thinking again about the first days with X Company, what did you hope for when you first came looking for work? What expectations did you have?

Added Information: More information on organization's charter. More information on respondent's level of aspiration. Insight into why people work.

Question 14: Thinking of today, what would you say are your present hopes and aspirations?

Added Information: Respondents views of mobility possibilities. Insight into respondent's level of aspiration, needs, and goals.

Question 15: Let's take a look at the contacts, if any, that you have with others while at work. How would you describe them?

Added Information: Insight into the feelings towards others in other work groups. May provide information about outside friendships. Insight into needs of employee such as need for isolation, alienation, etc. Insight into impact of informal group culture on respondent.

Question 16: I have worked in and conducted studies in a number of plants. There always seems to be quite a variety of types of friendships in the plant. How do you feel about the friendliness in this plant? Without mentioning names, would you please tell me if any of the employees in this plant are your own very close personal friends?

Added Information: May gain insight into degree of cohesiveness of employee groups. Insight into opportunity for human interaction. Insight into informal group culture. Insight into affiliation needs.

Question 17: How do the employees in your department feel about the management? For example, what sorts of things does management do that they like? Dislike?

Added Information: Insight into leadership patterns. Insight into employee criteria of effective leadership. Insight into respondent's dependency needs. Insight into pressures that may be felt by employees.

Question 18: Is there anything about your present job that you would like to see changed?

Added Information: Degree of ego-involvement in his work. Degree of identification with the health of the organization. Insight into any grievances.

Question 19: How do you think the employees in your department feel about the piece rates?

Added Information: Insight into impact of the incentive system. Insight into level of aspiration of respondent and his degree of involvement in quality and quantity of production.

Question 20: How do you think the employees in your department feel about working conditions?

Added Information: Insight into the nature of and degree of ego-involvement of the respondent in his work situations.

Question 21: How do you think the employees feel about quality on the job?

Added Information: Insight into degree of ego-involvement in health of the organization. Insight into the challenges and frustrations of the job. Impact of incentive system on controls.

Question 22: What would you say people in your department like best about X Company?

Added Information: Insight into the degree of ego-involvement in the company and the nature of the involvement. Insight into the respondent's needs, abilities, level of aspirations, and goals. Insight into the informal employee culture.

Question 23: Let's forget your job for the moment. I am trying to understand what sort of things people do once they get out of here at the end of the day. For example, what happens to you when you leave the plant at the end of the day?

Added Information: Insight into abilities, level of aspirations, affiliation needs, and goals of the respondent. Insight into the impact of the working world on the "outside world" and vice versa. Insight into the degree of ego-involvement in the company.

Question 24: What would you say the employees in your department liked least about X Company?

Added Information: Insight into the degree of ego-involvement in the company and the nature of this involvement. Insight into the respondent's needs, abilities, level of aspiration, and goals. Insight into the informal employee culture.

Question 25: From your point of view what do you think the company has a right to expect of you in return for the wages that they give you?

Added Information: Insight into the degree of ego-involvement in the health of the organization. Insight into the respondent's needs, level of aspiration, and values. Insight into management-employee relationships. Insight into informal employee culture.

Question 26: I should like to read some statements to you and ask you how you feel about them?

a) Being firm with the employees is the best way to insure that they will do a good job.

b) A foreman who keeps asking his men for their ideas on things is actually admitting he doesn't know his job.

c) It's smart for a foreman to constantly check up on the employees to see that they are doing a good job.[3]

Added Information: Insight into respondent's dependency needs. Insight into informal employee culture valuations of effective leadership. Insight into the quality of the management-employee relationship. Insight into respondent's view of how to lead his fellow employees.

Question 27: May I please ask you to focus again on yourself. I should like to read you some choices and ask you to choose those you prefer.

a) Do you prefer to be in a situation where you are directing others or do you prefer to be in a situation where you are doing your own job and receiving directions from others?

b) Do you prefer to have many and different things to do or do you prefer to have pretty much the same thing to do during the day?

c) Do you prefer to work by yourself or do you prefer to work with others?

Added Information: Insight into the degree of routineness or

---

[3] Questions 26 *a, b,* and *c* have been inspired by some interview sheets I saw belonging to the Survey Research Center, University of Michigan.

variety of the work. Insight into the level of aspiration for upward mobility.

Question 28: Do you have any way of knowing how management feels about the employees?

Added Information: Insight into the impact of the leadership patterns of the respondent. Insight into employee ego-involvement in the organization and his relationships with the management.

Question 29: Do you feel there is any pressure here to get out the work?

Added Information: Insight into degree of ego-involvement of respondent in the health of the company. Insight into the dependency needs of the respondent.

Question 30: Is there any thing that you would like to see the company communicate that it isn't communicating? In other words, is there any information the employees would like to have about the company that they do not have at the present time?

Added Information: Insight into the degree of ego-involvement of the respondent in the company. Insight into the employee's level of aspiration and goals.[4]

A Summary of the Internal Validity Checks

A matrix analysis of "the questions that validate other questions" and of the number of times a question is "checked" for validity is presented in Table 1.[5] We note that most questions tend to provide validity checks for at least four other questions. The range is from 4 to 9 questions. However, the same is not true when we note the number of times a given question is checked. We find, for example, that some questions are checked for validity only once whereas some are as high as 16 and 24 times. This is an imbalance the writer is trying to correct. Actually the three least "validated" questions are 12, 13, and 23. The first

---

[4] In addition to the standard questions above, at times other questions are added to satisfy the immediate needs of the organization as seen by management. This is done only if it does not jeopardize the research.

[5] The writer is indebted to Mr. Charles Brodigan for the table.

deals with the individual's original reason for joining the firm and the second deals with the original expectations he had about his work. The third deals with the respondent's present outside activities.

After the analysis above made the imbalance clear, the writer added four new questions, two of which relate to questions 12 and 13. Up to this point, another question to tap the outside activities that can pass the pretest has not been found. The writer is continuing to strive to find one.

One closely related point is that the researcher is nòt free to lengthen the list of questions indefinitely. At the moment it would

FIGURE 1

ANALYSIS OF VALIDITY CHECK

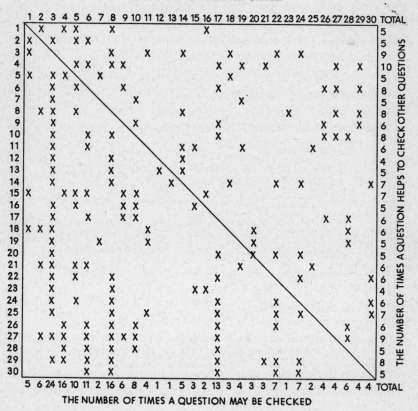

seem that 35 or perhaps even as many as 40 questions may be included in an interview. The criterion in the past has been to ask no more questions than will keep a respondent much more than an hour. This criterion is not very rigorous since some respondents may take as little as twenty minutes while others as much as three hours. (Both of these figures are unusual. Fifty to sixty-five minutes tends to be the mode.)

We turn now to how these questions are used in the interview situation. Let us assume that the researcher has left his university office, arrived at the location where interviews are to be held in the plant and is ready to begin.

The Interview

The Setting. The interviews are held preferably in surroundings familiar to the employees but safely away from interference and any kind of observation by others. In this case the interviews were held in a room that had once served as the office of a foreman in the factory. An old desk and two chairs were the only furnishing. (Actually a relatively new desk had been placed in the room but was "appropriated" by one of the foremen. He was kind enough to give the researcher the old desk.)

The room was easily accessible to the factory employees. More important, it permitted the interviews to be held in the factory. If the office used had been located in the white-collar area, the commonly observed status and symbolic difference between white- and blue-collar workers might make the factory and office employees feel quite uncomfortable.

The primitiveness of the room and its furniture probably helped to decrease the social gap between the researcher and the employees.

Overcoming the Social Distance between Researcher and Respondent. Some researchers believe that "getting down with the boys" by showing a willingness and a skill in swearing, drinking, etc., helps to establish proper rapport. The writer has attempted many of these activities and has concluded that it is not necessarily true. In fact, they may increase the distance between the researcher and the subject. One important reason is the expectations the employees have of research. If they view the role of the researcher as requiring "conservative," "mild" behavior; a swearing, down-to-earth approach may create more confusion than weld friendships. Employees tend to be especially defensive of academicians who they believe have much more education than they do. They are very sensitive to any behavior on the part of the researcher that they interpret as being "phony" and an attempt to become "one-of-the-boys." First of all such behavior may imply to the employee that the researcher really views himself as better or at least different. Second, if the researcher assumes that acting will gain his friendship he may be perceived by the employees as being disrespectful of them, their culture, and society. Research relationships are earned through integrated, congruent relationships and not by diplomatic playing of the role of a "good guy." In the writer's opinion, the subjects respect, above all, personal integrity. They do not tend to desire to communicate their personal feelings to an actor—especially one who behaves in a way that is not truly being himself.

There is another reason why the researcher should exercise caution in automatically assuming that being "one-of-the-boys" will help him. In many plants, as we shall see, as is true in this one, the employees do *not* share very important personal feelings with each other. Playing the role of "another employee" places the researcher, if successful, in a system of relationships where much important information that he is interested in is hardly ever discussed.

Note-Taking during the Interview.   This researcher finds it necessary to take notes during the interview. To date no respondents have overtly complained or manifested uncomfortableness because of the note-taking. On the contrary, if a helping relationship is established, the respondents tend to be quite co-operative. Many keep one eye on the researcher as he takes notes and are kind enough to slow down if they feel they are ahead of his writing. Upon questioning them, many respond that they would feel offended if notes are not taken. How else can the researcher record accurately what they have to say? Doesn't the researcher feel that their words are important? Moreover, as one respondent pointed out, "Don't you think your work is important enough to do it the right way?"

Some researchers report high success with a tape recorder. In the writer's experiences, the recorder has been most helpful with upper-level executives especially those who are quite verbal. In most other cases that he has experienced, the recorder seems to make the respondent uncomfortable. This, in turn, tends to make the researcher uncomfortable. The resulting tension may be either overtly or covertly communicated to, and picked up by, the respondent who, because of the research interview, may be especially "tuned" to receive such messages.

Much more research needs to be conducted before we will know with certainty the conditions under which each method is the most effective. Until then it is best that the researcher use those research methods with which he is comfortable. One guidepost that seems to hold for all cases is that no matter how "objective" the researcher believes his instruments to be, in most cases, the subjects do not tend to separate him from his instruments. If he is not comfortable in what he is doing, the subjects may tend to have difficulty in being fully functioning themselves.

Explaining the Research Project to Each Respondent. Partly to explain and partly to help establish the credibility and legitimacy of the research it seems useful to explore with the respondent before the interview such things as:

1. The objectives of the research.
2. How each party may profit from the research.
3. Why the researcher is conducting the research.
4. How does the researcher view his role?
5. What is the relationship between the organization, the researcher, and the subjects?
6. What is to happen to the results? If they are reported, how will they be reported?
7. What guarantees does the respondent have that his name will not be used?
8. How can the researcher be trusted?
9. How is each respondent selected?
10. Must the respondent answer all questions? Are there right and wrong answers?
11. How personal are the questions?

On the basis of our experiences, these questions are important for each respondent. If the researcher covers them at his own initiative, he may help to give the respondent the feeling that the researcher truly understands and cares for him. The respondent may appreciate the researcher's initiative because it may not be easy for him to feel free to ask such questions.

Below is a verbatim transcript of how the writer introduces himself to each respondent at the outset of an interview.[6]

Good morning, won't you come in and sit down. (Sits down.) My name is Chris Argyris. I teach and I do research at Yale University. You might wonder why in heavens name is Yale University interested in doing this kind of research. Well, the answer is simple. Yale University has had a long tradition of trying to teach as realistically and as concretely as it can what are the major problems people face in trying to get out the goods, in trying to manage plants. It's especially important for us to keep in touch with the real world because we not only have young men going out, but we have many of our alumni who come back for courses and they are especially pleased to see that the teaching is being kept up to date with facts of life.

As a result of this most of us who teach at the university continually conduct research. Also many of us have worked in industry. The organization with which I'm affiliated has conducted research in many organizations such as banks, insurance companies, telephone companies, automobile plants, electrical manufacturing and so on. About a year ago we realized that we had never studied the manufacturer of . . .

As a result we decided that this industry would be our next study. We made a tour of a number of different corporations, and for many reasons selected X Corporation. We had a long visit with the president. In effect we said the following to him: Look Mr. President, we should like to make a proposition for you to consider. We should like the opportunity to talk with all the employees on all levels in a particular plant of your corporation. What we hope to get out of it is a better understanding of the human problems that industry faces in order that we can be effective teachers and in order that we contribute more to the knowledge of healthy organizations. Therefore,

---

[6] This introduction was given to the management in groups. Any questions that arose were then answered. The discussions were lively and each lasted about two hours. As a result the material did not have to be repeated for the management at the beginning of each interview. In the case of the employees, the management felt it would be too costly to have such meetings. Consequently the introduction was repeated in every interview.

it's our hope to publish a couple of articles or perhaps even a book as a result of the study.

In return for this opportunity Yale University (through a grant received from the National Institute of Mental Health) will pay for much of the cost of the project plus it promises to provide the organization with a feed back of the results.

When the president heard this, he sounded quite interested. He remarked that they were always interested in trying to better understand how people really felt about their company.

We responded that we were happy to hear that they were interested. However, before they made a decision we thought we should let them know some of the conditions that we must lay down because we are a university research group. The first condition is that under no circumstances would we report anybody's name, be he manager or employee in any kind of a written or oral report to anybody in the organization. The only kind of reporting of results would be by department. Moreover, we would not interview and report about a department that had less than five or six people. We want to guarantee complete anonymity.

What do we plan to put in our report? In your department we would say, for example, 10 per cent of the people answered question number 1 in this way, 20 per cent did that way, and so on. In other words, all we intend to do is to provide the percentages with some sort of organized manner to come up with our view of the company.

The other requirement is that under no circumstances can we permit management to select the people that we interview. This of course leads to the question of how you were selected, and you might wonder how you were picked because not everybody in your department was picked to be interviewed. The answer is really quite simple. Many years ago, we found out that if we permitted management to select the employees, those that came up to be interviewed felt, "My god, why did they select me, are they worried about me?" Worse yet, we found out that those not selected were even more anxious, and they felt that this showed that management had no interest in them and that there might be a possibility of their being fired. In order to prevent any of this unnecessary worry we make it a strict rule that we select the employees.

Therefore, in the case of your department I have a list of all the employees in the department. I decided, based on our rules, that I needed 25 people out of 40. I took all the names and had them typed on a slip of paper, put them in a box and then had someone pick 25 names. In other words, you were picked at random.

You might also wonder that it's easy for us to say that we promise no names will be mentioned but after all, how do you know this, how can you trust me? The truth of the matter is you've never met me before and of course you have no way of knowing you can trust me any more, frankly, than I know that you will tell me honestly how you and others feel about what is going on in your department. This is a problem that I realize we in research have and I don't want to skirt it. I should like to try to tackle my side of this problem as follows: Let's assume for a moment that I was a liar, a diplomatic liar, but nevertheless a liar. A person who would go up to a manager and say, do you know what so and so really thinks of you. Now in my experience I would predict two things would happen. First the grapevine would find out and this would immediately make the employees feel quite negative towards me. If somehow the grapevine clogged up, then if management took any action, they know that they had communicated this information only to Chris and therefore would know exactly where to place the blame. The resulting uproar would probably get me kicked out as it rightly should. I would then have a problem because when Yale University would ask me how was the investment coming along, I'd have an awful time trying to provide them a satisfactory answer. In other words, we make sure that no one's name is mentioned, not only for their good, but especially for our own good.

We don't ask any personal questions, or try to ask any question about specific individuals and place anybody on the spot. In fact, you might like to know that the same kinds of questions we ask you we ask everybody else from the president on down.

I think that's about the end of my speech. I've talked quite a bit, perhaps you have some questions you would like to ask me?

Dealing with the Researcher.   The researcher is a stranger to the employees; a stranger who intends to ask questions. Even though the employees may feel they want to co-operate, they may have some problems of adapting to the researcher.

Sometimes the employees will tend to adapt by deliberately trying to bait the researcher. They may try to get the researcher to tell them about the private discussions that the researcher has had with top management (and vice versa). If the researcher breaks his professional confidences, he will only tend to harm his position. As one foreman once suggested, "If you tell us how the boss feels (even the good things) what guarantee do we have that you will not tell the boss how we feel?"

At other times, the employees may poke fun at the researcher.

For example, the first few men of one department came into the office and introduced themselves by asking if the researcher were "Mike Wallace." In another department the researcher received an envelope which contained a set of paper dolls with a note reading "to the brain shrinker." In still another department the men heard that the department's scapegoat (an elderly lady with low intelligence) was to be interviewed. The employees hazed her by telling her that she would be placed on a desk, that hot towels would be placed on her head and that she would be shocked by an electric current. The respondent arrived at the office shaking like a leaf. After careful support and questioning the respondent admitted her plight. The researcher was then able to help set the respondent at ease. In the writer's opinion, such an incident should *not* be discussed further with management. These situations are symptomatic of how some employees (a minority) cope with the researcher. They should be respected by the researcher with the same professional rules that he applies to other data. If he were to make a complaint to the management in order to prevent further occurrences, the researcher could, as one man said, "Be placed on our s___ list."

Care should be taken, however, to help the individual involved to release his or her tension. In all such cases that the writer has experienced (and these have been very few) the respondents have been able to carry on and provide important information.

Maintaining a Professional Role. Many times respondents intentionally or unintentionally try to make the researcher violate some of his basic rules of professional conduct. At times respondents may try to induce the researcher to tell them what others have already said in previous interviews. Some do this quite directly. For example, "Tell me, before I begin, what sorts of things have the boys been telling you?" Still others are much more indirect, "I bet you have found the boys quite helpful, heh, Doc? They tell you every thing?" In both cases the researcher may respond "The people are most co-operative and I am learning quite a bit; however, as I promised you, I cannot discuss what others have said any more than I will tell the others what you say."

Another example is as follows:

SHE: I betcha a lot of people have been complaining about wages.
RESEARCHER: People have certainly been most co-operative in saying how they feel.

In this way the researcher prevents himself from being induced to say anything about what other people have told him. At times employees unknowingly ask a question that violates the professional role. The following incident is taken from one of the interviews.

RESPONDENT: Tell me did the other boys tell you that we lost our old foreman, did the boys tell you?
RESEARCHER: I really can't answer that because as I promised I can't tell anyone what they said in the interview.
RESPONDENT: Well, let me put it this way, do you know that we lost our foreman?
RESEARCHER: Thanks for helping me I would say I now know that you have lost your foreman.

Employees have, at times, insisted that the researcher place in his report a personal quote with their name attached because, as one put it, "I want them to know exactly how I feel." In all cases the researcher should not make such promises because he could easily be viewed by every respondent as a tool to resolve their personal problems.

Other employees have asked if the researcher can guarantee that a particular thing they have said would be quoted. In such cases, a useful reply is, "As I mentioned before, I can only report major trends. It is difficult for me to tell you if your views will be quoted because I do not know the trends. In any case, if your views are mentioned, may I add that your name will not be identified with them."

"Can you tell when people are lying?" is another very frequently asked question by respondents who are probably ambivalent as to how they should answer the questions. The researcher may find it useful to reply, "Yes, after interviewing so many people, we can pretty much tell when they are not telling what they feel is the truth. Also we have ways to check the consistency of their answers. Once in a while a person prefers not to participate but is unable to say so. Maybe he or she feels quite embarrassed.

We never stop that person and point out to him that we feel he is lying. We continue as if all is well but are very careful not to include his interview with the others."

Still other employees try to obtain from the researcher some assurance that the feedback of the information will be of help to them in obtaining what they desire. The researcher may not guarantee anything to anyone except an honest feedback of the results. He can add, if it is true, that the management is aware that it would be a poor policy to involve the employees in a study if they had no intentions of making any reasonable changes that are suggested by the employees.

Dealing with the Reticent Respondent. If an employee, upon entering the interview situation, announces that he hasn't any intention (or prefers not) to answer any questions, the researcher must always respect this desire. Every interviewee has the right to reject the interviewer and the interview. Not only is this a moral right, but it is a scientific requirement. An employee who prefers not to talk will only tend to be highly defensive and probably provide data that are distorted if urged to talk. Under such conditions the researcher should first reward the employee for feeling free to be honest. "Above all Mr. So and So I want you to know that it makes me feel good to hear you say what you truly feel. I do not, nor does the organization, want you to be interviewed against your wishes. How would you like to handle this problem? Would you like to leave now? May I suggest that the others in your department might wonder why you left so early. Perhaps we can sit here and talk about the weather or something for a few minutes. However you decide is fine with me."

The writer has been faced with a reticent employee twice in his experience. The first time the employee decided to talk about baseball and in fifteen minutes asked the writer to ask him the questions. The second one left in fifteen minutes and never asked for a return appearance.

The more difficult situation occurs when the employee refuses to go to the interviewing room. The refusal tends to be public and the management without the researcher's knowledge may try to coerce the employee to be interviewed. This has happened once to the writer. The management in that particular situation interpreted the behavior as insubordination. The management informed the researcher of the difficulties since the researcher had to select someone else. The researcher helped the management to realize that he did not interpret such behavior as insubordination, although he could understand how they would. No attempt was made by the researcher to communicate these feelings directly to the reticent employee. If the researcher had made such an attempt he would have in effect placed himself in the organizational power structure. Of course, he may ask management's permission to communicate his feelings to the employee. However, such direct contact could easily be interpreted by the management as the researcher competing for the employee's favor. Some may wonder if the other employees may not like to see the researcher communicate directly to the employee in question. In the one situation, the employees (later on) admitted they would have liked to see the researcher contact the employee but realized this was difficult because, as they saw it, the employee did not want to see the researcher. Thus a refusal to follow up was interpreted by the other employees as a sign of respect for the reticent employee's feelings.

It is hoped that the information above provides the reader with insight into how this researcher conducts his research interviews. No claim is made that the "right approach" is to be found in the material above. It *is* suggested that the research techniques used should not only be influenced by a theory but they should be a highly personal decision related to how the researcher feels he can maximize his role.

CHAPTER

III

The Analysis of the Data

LET US NOW assume that the interviews have been held and we are ready for the analysis of the data.

As in the choice of diagnostic procedures, the theoretical framework, and the theoretical guideposts (discussed in Chapter I) provide the basic guides for the methods to analyze the data.

A Possible Model for Analyzing an Organization

We begin with the contribution of the theoretical framework. It provides the researcher with four basic analytical categories to guide him in the analysis.[1] They are:

1. The demands made of the participant by the formal organization (includes demands from the job, the formal policies and practices).
2. The predispositions that the participants may wish to express while participating in the organization.
3. The informal activities that the employees create to adapt to the formal organization.
4. The administration's reaction to the informal activities.

The theoretical guideposts provide clues as to how the four basic categories above are to be analyzed and conceptualized. For

---

[1] These five variables are broken down in detail in Chris Argyris, *Personality and Organization* (New York: Harper & Bros., 1957). Again we remind the reader that the approach does not presume to include variables "outside" the plant context. Such variables must be included if the theory above is to become more general.

63

example, from the definition of organization we derive that each category should be conceptualized as an organic part of the organization. It also follows from the definition, that we must ascertain (1) the *objective* of each part, (2) the interrelationship of the parts that create a *pattern,* and (3) the processes by which the pattern becomes *self-maintaining.*

The problem of selecting a model is indeed a difficult one. The very fact of utilizing the English language as part of the model oversimplifies the analysis since our language forces us to think in linear terms. The model that is needed is one that may conceptually describe a reality that is much more complex. As Arber states, "A written account is a mere thread, spun artificially into a chain-like form, whereas the weft of thought from which it is derived, the elements are interconnected according to a more complex mode." [2]

In requiring that the model should not do violence to the complexity and uniqueness of the organization being studied, we assume that the construction of the model should take as its guide the complexity of the data and not necessarily some values one has about the nature of rigorous models. Making the model "subservient" to the data leads, at this time, to the development of a rather simple gross model which lacks the desired rigor, but perhaps it can be considered respectable for a researcher to let reality be his guide in choosing a model. Philip M. Morse makes the point that to understand certain problems, one must understand the pattern before the details.[3] Slowly, as Kurt Lewin suggests, by successive approximations, a rigorous model will someday be evolved.[4] Once one has "arrived" by this path, one will not have to "return" to try to do something about variables left out.[5] Holding the above hypothesis, one may turn to Karl W.

---

[2] Agnes Arber, *The Mind and the Eye* (Cambridge University Press, 1954), p. 46.

[3] Philip M. Morse, "Statistics and Operations Research," *Operations Research,* Vol. IV, No. 4 (February, 1956).

[4] Kurt Lewin, *A Dynamic Theory of Personality* (New York, McGraw-Hill Book Co., Inc., 1935).

[5] For an interesting article related to this problem, see John L. Kennedy, "A 'Transition-Model' Laboratory for Research on Cultural Change," *Human Organization,* Vol. XIV (Fall, 1955), pp. 16–18.

Deutsch's definitions of a model as a useful point of departure. Deutsch defines a model as a "structure of symbols and operating rules which is supposed to match a set of relevant points in an existing structure of process." [6]

The model used here is borrowed (more in spirit than in substance) from the physical sciences. It is the model of a system with an input, an output, and feedback to the input. This basic pattern is all that we may borrow. Nevertheless, the model will be useful as a device to help organize the complexity, lead to new insights, and make a few qualitative predictions.[7] As C. W. Churchman, R. L. Ackoff, and E. L. Arnoff suggest all useful models are not necessarily mathematical nor are they used for accurate prediction or calculation. There are many that in essence are diagrams enabling the researcher to bring together, from many different fields, knowledge about organization. They help to separate the trivial from the relevant.[8] In the field of organizational behavior, where the researcher is constantly overwhelmed by the richness, depth, and complexity of the variables, such aid is not to be taken lightly.

Problems in Understanding Predispositions in Field Research

Let us turn to the first category that requires study, namely, the predisposition of the subject.

First a predisposition is defined as a tendency to act in a particular manner under specific conditions. The concept predisposition is an inferred "stirred-up" condition of the organism in relationship to some stimulus in the environment. Predispositions are not conceived as "in" the body or "in" the environment. They are interactional concepts hypothesized in order to understand the transaction or interpenetration between the individual and the social system. It should be made clear that a predisposition is not assumed to be as the "need" or "need systems" postu-

---

[6] Karl W. Deutsch, "On Communication Models in the Social Sciences," *Public Opinion Quarterly,* Vol. XVI (1952), pp. 356–80.

[7] See Deutsch's article cited above for an interesting discussion of the different functions a model may serve.

[8] C. W. Churchman, R. L. Ackoff, and E. L. Arnoff, *Introduction to Operations Research* (New York: John Wiley & Sons, Inc., 1957), p. 71.

lated by many psychologists. Their concept usually refers to phenomena that are more genotypic than that to which we refer. The predisposition is inferred by the analyst by combing the interview for any themes from which he can infer the desires that the participant wishes to satisfy while at work.

A word about the problem of diagnosing predispositions in an organizational setting. It has been (and continues to be) the writer's desire to develop (or use already developed) personality tests which can be administered to employees of an organization. The results of the tests can serve as independent validity checks of the predispositions. This desire to date has not been fulfilled especially as it is related to understanding the predispositions of the lower-level employees. After a lengthy search the writer selected and used three different tests (two semiprojective and one objective) to study the aspects of the personality of the employees. All three met with resounding hostility and other types of resistance from the lower-level employees. The employees were apparently quite threatened. One reason, we now hypothesize, is that many of the employees have lived, and continue to live, in a world in which their personal self is not considered as important as their contribution to the business. As Wilensky and Lebeaux point out in a factory "who you are" becomes much less important than "what you can do." [9] Forcing them to take a look at aspects of their personalities may then be a threatening experience for them. A challenge of the future for clincal psychologists is to create a personality test which will not make an employee (who is *not* necessarily interested in focusing upon his personality) so defensive that he refuses to take it. At least on an overt level not too much difficulty is experienced with high-level executives or staff experts such as engineers, scientists, etc.

The Potency of the Predispositions

Every individual has a number of predispositions that he wants to express while a member of the organization, each of which may vary in degree of importance (or potency). The po-

---

[9] Harold L. Wilensky, and Charles W. Lebeaux, *Industrialization and Social Welfare* (New York: Russell Sage Foundation, November, 1944), p. 43.

tency of each predisposition may vary from individual to individual and within the same individual at different times in his life or different situations.

The degree of importance of each predisposition may be arbitrarily assigned the following numbers. Zero for no importance; one for regular importance (RI); two for high importance (HI); and four for extremely high importance (EHI).

The potency of each predisposition is ascertained by the analyst who goes through each interview looking for content from which he can infer a predisposition plus its degree of importance for the individual.

Standard scoring procedures are being developed in order to decrease as much as possible (which at this point is by no means enough) the subjective guesswork on the part of the analyst. The procedures are still quite crude and require further refinement. It is presented in order to provide the reader with an idea of the direction toward which the scoring procedures are developing.

A score of one is assigned to those predispositions that are inferred from replies to question 2, 4, 6, 7, 9, and 10 because the researcher indirectly induces the respondent to talk about those aspects of himself. Predispositions inferable from the replies to questions 5, 12, 13, and 16 receive a score of two because they are not induced by the researcher. They are presumed to be more important because the respondent takes the initiative to mention them.[10] The assumption is that the spontaneous mentioning of a predisposition implies that it is more potent for the individual. Responses related to predispositions in questions 22 and 24 receive a score of three because they purport to top the most crucial aspects for the employee. Normally the remaining questions would not provide personality information about predispositions. If they do, the predispositions inferred would be assigned a score of two since they are spontaneous.

Using the above scoring schedule the analyst combs each inter-

---

[10] The writer is not pleased with this assumption. Some of the most important predispositions may not be immediately conscious. We are working on a new scoring procedure designed to eliminate this and other flaws. However, we did operate with this assumption during the research reported here.

view for all the predispositions that the respondent mentions directly or indirectly. As he discovers a predisposition, he lists it on a work sheet on which he will construct a frequency distribution. A single line is placed next to it if mentioning the predisposition was induced by the researcher. A double score (2) is placed next to a predisposition every time it is mentioned spontaneously by the respondent without any prompting from the interviewer. A score of three is placed next to a predisposition mentioned or inferable in questions 22 or 24. These questions purport to tap "the most important" aspects of a respondent's work life. The analyst ends up with a list of the predispositions on the left-hand side of his work sheet plus a simple frequency distribution of checks for each predisposition. These checks are totaled for each predisposition. A score of four is assigned to that predisposition (or predispositions) receiving the highest score. These predispositions are assigned an Extremely High Importance or potency (EHI). High Importance (HI) with a score of two is assigned to all those predispositions that cluster on the next lower mode in the frequency distribution. The remaining predispositions are assigned Regular Importance (RI) with a score of one.

For the purposes of an operational validity check of the potency score, a random sample of interviews was given to two trained social scientists who had never seen the data before. They were asked to infer the potency for each factor using the scoring procedure above. The agreement between their two sets of scores was 70 per cent and the agreement of each with the author was

TABLE 1

A SAMPLE PREDISPOSITION WORK SHEET

Predisposition	Frequency of Mention	Totals	Potency
Alone	1111	4	Regular
Control	⊞1	6	High
Togetherness	⊞ 11	7	High
Wages	⊞ ⊞	10*	Extremely high
Routine	111	3	Regular
Directive	1	1	Regular

* If togetherness had received a score of nine then it would have been assigned an extremely high potency as long as no predisposition had a score of eight. In other words, there must be a minimum gap of two points between high potency and extremely high potency categories.

68 and 72 per cent respectively (after a learning period of four hours).

Samples of Interviews

In order to help clarify the scoring procedures some verbatim examples are presented below of the answers given to ten (out of a total of thirty) questions. One interview will represent responses of an individual with a low and one with a high self-actualizing score.

Because of the commitments made to each respondent that a total interview would never be published, the material below represents a composite picture of several interviews. One reply representing a particular question is taken from each interview. Therefore, ten interviews are sampled representing low and high views of individuals with low and high actualizing scores.

A sample interview of an individual with a high self-actualizing score is presented first. The question being discussed is noted in the left hand column. The middle column presents the actual verbatim material. In the right hand column two bits of data are present. They are the interviewer's inference of the predisposition(s) expressed by the verbatim material and his inference as to the degree to which the predisposition can be expressed in the situation. These latter inferences are totaled and the average provides the researcher's inference as to the "actual degree of expression" the respondent experiences with a given predisposition. The exact manner the actual expression scores are used is found in Chapter IV.[11]

COMPOSITE INTERVIEW OF INDIVIDUALS WITH
HIGH SELF-ACTUALIZING SCORES

Question		*Predisposition*	*Inferred Expression*
2	*How would you describe your job? Would you say it is routine, monotonous, different, full of variety?*		

---

[11] The interviews are selected from the study of Plant Y reported in Chapter V.

Question		Predis- position	Inferred Expression
	There isn't much variety in my job. I do pretty much the same thing. There's an over-all routine you might say with variety once in a while.	Routine	3
	RESEARCHER: What are your feelings about the degree of variety you get on the job.		
	RESPONDENT: Fine, excellent. I can make good pay if I have the same thing to do. I don't want a job with too much variety.		
3	*What personal satisfactions, if any, can a person obtain from a job like yours?*		
	I like to be my own boss and to do a good job. I guarantee my work and that's why I've got a good job. If there is anything bad, I do it again at no expense to them. Also I like to be my own boss. They don't worry about me, and I give them a good day's work with good quality.	High quality Control	2 3
6	*If you were hiring a foreman for a department like yours, what kind of a foreman would you hire? How do you feel a good foreman behaves?*		
	I think he should co-operate with the men. He should be able to work things out so that everybody is working steady and making a buck. After all, that's why we're all here. We got a good foreman. He sees to it that we're kept busy, he keeps out of our	Wages Control	3 3

Question		Predis-position	Inferred Expression
	hair, and isn't a complete company man. If he's just been chewed out by a guy upstairs about quality or something, we never get it. He knows our main job is to make a buck.	Non-involve-ment	3
7	*How do you think the employees in your department feel about a kitty? How important would you say is the kitty?*		
	I think all men like to have a kitty. The way it is set up now it is impossible to have one. It used to be when you had a kitty you felt pretty good because if you didn't feel too good one day or do too well, you knew that you could make it up. But now you worry.	Control	0
	Well, I think the fellows just accepted that the kitty had to go. I hated to see them go but I can see the company's point of view. So now, I give them a day's work, and they don't bother me with company headaches.	Non-involve-ment	3
8	*In answering the next question please feel free if you wish not to limit yourself to your job. Let us focus on you as an individual. What would you say are your important abilities? What are the things you feel you can do well?*		
	I enjoy my work. I can make just about anything in this division. It feels good to put out something you can look at and be proud. I'm going to hate the	Gener-alist	3

Question	*Predis-position*	*Inferred Expression*

day when quality goes out the window. That day is beginning to come—they're pushing for low cost and high output. — High-quality work — 2

10   *How do you feel about the trips the top brass make throughout the plant stopping and saying hello to people?*

They never bother me. I never see them. They leave me alone. I don't know anything about them and glad (laughs). I don't want them to bring their troubles to me. — Non-involve-ment — 3

14   *Thinking of today, what would you say are your present hopes and aspirations?*

I'm satisfied. After all, what I'm working for is a buck. That's what counts. — Wages — 3

RESEARCHER: Would you like to be a foreman?

RESPONDENT: Oh no! Not for me. I have a few friends and I want to keep them. Responsibility is a lousy thing to have, Mister. You can't make anyone happy. — Non-involve-ment — 3

16   *How friendly would you say the people are in this plant?*

I like the people around here. They're very friendly. Nice folks.

RESEARCHER: Could you help me understand what you mean by friendly people?

Question		Predis- position	Inferred Expression
	RESPONDENT: Sure—you know—they're friendly people—you know—well, how to put it (hm, hm). Well, friendly people. You know, they leave you alone, and I leave them alone. We get along very well.	Together- ness	3
17	*How do the employees in your department feel about management?*		
	They're wonderful people. The thing I like about this plant is that there is no pressure. People aren't down your neck all the time. They come around, say hello, they are sincerely interested in your gripes if you have any. Good management, I'd say.	Control	3
22	*What would you say people in your department like best about Plant —?*		
	No pressure and the high wages. That's what I like. But if I had to choose, no doubt about it; the good wages. That's one thing this company is known for. Even during the depression they paid good wages.	Control Wages	3 3

COMPOSITE INTERVIEW OF INDIVIDUALS WITH
LOW SELF-ACTUALIZING SCORES

2	*How would you describe your job? Would you say it is routine, monotonous, different, full of variety?*		

Question		Predis-position	Inferred Expression
	Well, I'd say my job has variety. It's not a run-of-the-mill job where you can go bats.	Variety	2
	RESEARCHER: Could you give me an idea of how much variety you feel the job has?		
	RESPONDENT: Oh, I'd say it's O.K. It's not as much as I'd like, I'd guess I'd say.		
3	*What personal satisfactions, if any, can a person obtain from a job like yours?*		
	I'd like to do a good job, but you can't do that in this outfit. I don't see any satisfactions except the almighty buck and that ain't as high as it should be. It used to be you could be your own boss. Now they pressure the living hell out of you. Pressure, pressure— that's all they give away these days.	Control Wages	0 1
6	*If you were hiring a foreman for a department like yours, what kind of a foreman would you hire? How do you feel a good foreman behaves?*		
	A good foreman ought to be able to satisfy the management and the guys in the shop. He should understand the workingman's view. We don't want much. We want a decent salary and we get that some of the time. We don't want to be hounded. A good foreman leaves me alone but sees to it that I have enough good jobs to make a good day's pay.	Wages Control	2 3

Question	*Predis-position*	*Inferred Expression*
RESEARCHER: How would you say the fellows feel about your foreman?		
RESPONDENT: I don't know. If you want to know how I feel, I'll tell you. I think he's a hell of a nice guy. He tries to do his best. Frankly, I'd hate to be in his boots. He takes a lot of shit from everybody. But he leaves us alone. I know he gets pressured from the brass, but he never pushes that crap on us. That's a good foreman. The guys bitch upstairs about something, but he doesn't come down hollering at us. All he ever asks us to do is to produce.	Non-involve-ment	3
7 *How do you think the employees in your department feel about a kitty? How important would you say is the kitty?*		
Kitties are damned important. Kitties used to be pretty good. Ten years ago it wasn't unheard of to have a thousand dollars. Five years ago, five hundred. Today if you've got twenty-five dollars, you're doing well. Tomorrow you don't even know what the hell you will do. Maybe you can make a day's pay. Maybe you can't. It's not like the old days when you were your own boss. Then you didn't worry. Now you worry all the time.	Need for control Wages	0 1
8 *In answering the next question please feel free if you wish not*		

Question	Predis-position	Inferred Expression

to limit yourself to your job. Let us focus on you as an individual. What would you say are your important abilities? What are the things you feel you can do well?

| Well, I'm a fix-it man. I can fix anything you can bring to my shop. I like to work with gadgets and make them run again. And I like to do a good job. None of this half-ass stuff to me. I like to look at something I've made or fixed and say—brother, *I* made that. Damn good quality. Times have changed. People don't look for quality as much. The company doesn't really care for the old high quality. The same at work. I like to do three or four different jobs and do it well. That's the hell of it—not like the old days when you could have many different jobs to do. | Generalist

High quality | 1

1 |

| **10** | *How do you feel about the trips the top brass make throughout the plant stopping and saying hello to people?* | | |

| | It's all right. I don't think it does very much harm if the fellows know it before he comes down. Also, they shouldn't spend too much time with people. A friendly hello and that's fine. What I want from them is to let me alone and give me no gas about the company. They worry about running the place and I get a day's pay for a day's work. They're always coming in and giving me the business about the | Non-involve-ment

Control | 1

1 |

Question	*Predis-position*	*Inferred Expression*

company. Who are they kiddin' —this place isn't going to go bankrupt.

14   *Thinking of today, what would you say are your present hopes and aspirations?*

When I was young I was naive. I came here figuring I'd be something. You know, become a supervisor or even a superintendent. I learned quick. You got no college education; you ain't going to get anywheres. So I forgot about it. Now all I want is to give them a good day's work and they give me my pay and no headaches. None of this damn pressure that they're putting on lately.

	Predisposition	Inferred Expression
	Upward mobility	0
	Wages	2
	Non-involvement	1
	Control	1

16   *How friendly would you say the people are in this plant?*

Things are not too friendly here —but that's O.K. Course the guys don't want to get too chummy. If everybody knew what everybody else is making, then you don't know if one guy comes up to you and wants you to give him the easy job you have. You understand me? People say hello—you know they pass the time of day—but I don't think they're real close. And as I told you before, that's O.K. by me.

	Predisposition	Inferred Expression
	Togetherness	3

17   *How do the employees in your department feel about management?*

Question		Predis-position	Inferred Expression
	The management? They don't impress me one way or the other. I'd be happy if they just stayed the hell out of the department. Left us alone and don't come around trying to act friendly. I heard one of them tell another guy that Company X was his (employees') company. Vo voom! Imagine that. If he'd a told me that I would tell him to shove—and you know where. Not me—I don't want to go home with any worries—not me. They come around to give me the business, but I don't listen— just nod and smile. Stay loose, I say, stay loose. All they want to do—apply the old pressure.	Non-involve-ment Control	2 1
22	*What would you say people in your department like best about Plant —?*		
	That's a good question. I some-times wonder. I guess I like the pay and the hours. I'd hate to be in another plant where I would have to work the night shift. Not that I am making all I should, but what I am making is O.K. But I'll tell you something, Mis-ter, I don't like this goddam pressure that's been hitting us the last six months or so. Not a bit.	Wages	2

The Predispositions of the Employees

Let us now describe the actual predispositions found to exist for the participants of this organization. The predispositions will be presented for four different organizational groupings. They are high-skilled factory employees (A), low-skilled factory employees (B), office employees (C), and management (D).

Before the results for each group are presented the definitions of the predispositions seem advisable.

Definition of Predisposition

The need to experience:

Togetherness in relation to the other employees. The feeling that the employees like each other without knowing each other or experiencing close human relationships. The emphasis is on skin-surface signs of friendliness.

Wages guaranteeing a fair standard of living and a secure job. The level of wages desired is that comparable for similar work in the community. The degree of *Job security* desired is having a permanent job during the most difficult depression periods that the employee experiences.

Noninvolvement in the formal activities of the organization excepting one's own specific job. This does not include the individual's attitude toward productivity. It includes such needs as being uninterested in upward mobility, unconcerned about the financial health of the organization, etc.

Control over one's own immediate work environment. This includes the need to be left alone by the boss and not to be pressured by the managerial controls and the formal policies and practices.

Passiveness in relation to the boss and the demands of the organization. Preferring to receive direction rather than direct others.

Aloneness in relation to the other employees. The need to have (ideally) no interactions with other employees.

Variety in one's work. The need to perform many and different tasks while at work.

Routine in one's work. The need to perform few and similar tasks while at work.

Higher wages than those presently receiving. Present wages are viewed as unjust.

High-quality work—the desire to aspire toward high-quality workmanship.

Directive toward others. The desire to initiate action for others.

Generalist in one's work. The desire to perform at a high level of proficiency all the jobs within the job family that one works.

TABLE 2

PRIMARY PREDISPOSITIONS OF EMPLOYEES IN
DEPARTMENTS A, B, AND C
Degree of Importance
Per Cent (N = 154)

Predisposition	Regular	High	Extremely High	Total
Togetherness	42.0	31.0	19.0	92.0
Wages	16.0	36.0	39.0	91.0
Noninvolvement	16.0	35.0	39.0	90.0
Control	31.0	35.0	23.0	89.0
Passive	65.0	1.0		66.0
Alone	29.0	32.0	4.0	65.0
Variety	48.0	6.0	2.0	56.0
Routine	53.0			53.0

TABLE 3

PRIMARY PREDISPOSITIONS OF FOREMEN
Degree of Importance
Per Cent (N = 30)

Predisposition	Regular	High	Extremely High	Total
Higher wages	10.0	33.0	54.0	97.0
Noninvolvement	54.0	20.0	17.0	91.0
Control	7.0	28.0	54.0	89.0
Variety	20.0	34.0	34.0	88.0
Togetherness	20.0	33.0	27.0	80.0
Directive	20.0	30.0	30.0	80.0

THE SYSTEM OF PLANT X [12]

Now that we have insight into the predispositions of the participants let us integrate this knowledge with the information that

[12] For a complete analysis a discussion like this one would be required for every department. Then the subsystems could be compared to the whole. In order to save space this discussion is concerned primarily with the high and low skilled workers and the management. This group comprises the majority of the employees.

is required in order to develop an understanding of the whole organization. As mentioned in the previous chapter, this includes information about (1) formal organization, (2) leadership, (3) managerial controls, and (4) "human controls." A model is presented below that attempts to organize the content known about these five categories of variables plus the interrelationships into the self-maintaining pattern or system that is the basic property of organization (see Figure 2).

The Intake

All systems are assumed to have "openings" where inputs can be brought into the system. In the case of Plant X the intake activities are conducted in the personnel department (which is located away from the plant). There all prospective employees are carefully interviewed and screened. From interviews with the personnel interviewers we learn that all applicants are evaluated for such factors as "neatness," "seriousness of purpose," a "desirable amount of humility," etc. The applicant is judged by the interviewer on these factors primarily during the interview and by the previous work record. As to the latter, if the applicant has a long list of jobs and cannot give an adequate explanation, he is considered a poor risk.

The employees usually hired are those who seem to be willing (1) to learn their new job reasonably quickly, (2) to produce adequately, (3) to attend regularly and on time, (4) to complain minimally, (5) to get along with the management and the employees, and (6) to view his job as a long-range commitment.

In short, the primary function of the personnel department is to make certain that only those employees enter the system who will not upset it. In this light, the function of personnel is to make certain no one is hired who might someday raise questions with the system. Since no formal tests are used for the evaluation, the success or failure depends upon the subjective skills of the personnel people. Judging from management's satisfaction with the employees, the personnel people must have developed unconsciously an uncanny subjective "feel" for those applicants who probably will be willing to accept the system and for those

FIGURE 2

THE SOCIAL SYSTEM OF PLANT X

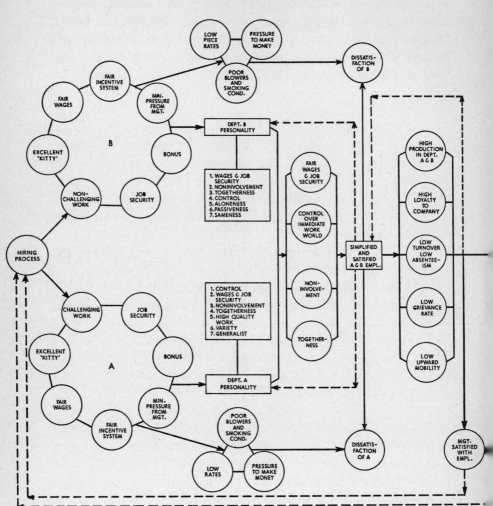

who will not. As we shall see in a moment, the management speaks highly of the employees in the plant. They especially like them because they are not "troublemakers." This raises the interesting possibility that effective personnel people, in this company, are those who have come to internalize the system and therefore, are capable of sensing someone who may not be loyal to the system. Such a diagnostic skill, although difficult to make explicit would no doubt be of great assistance to the organization and the individual. It will tend to prevent individuals from entering a system that will not be able to accept them and thereby help to assure organizational equilibrium. It will also tend to prevent the individual from having to go through the

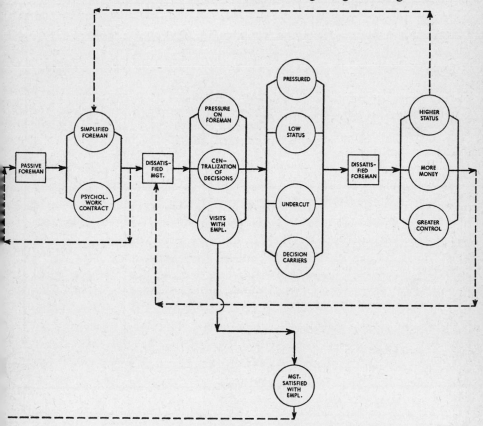

negative process of being dissatisfied in the system which eventually may lead him to consider the difficult action of leaving. All these are simply speculations that require further research if systematic answers are to be obtained.

The Formal Requirements of the High-Skilled Subsystem A

The individual passes through the intake process and enters one of two subsystems; the low skill or high skill. If the individual enters the high-skill subsystem (A), he enters a world which according to the respondents has the following characteristics:

a) Challenging Work. Eighty-three per cent of the employees in A report that they gain much personal satisfaction while working because they have challenging and creative work. Ninety-four per cent describe their work as having "plenty of variety" or "as much variety as they can handle or more." A few qualitative examples are:

I think the satisfaction I get is to know that I have done a job well. I like to do a perfect job; I like to feel something's really good; it's really perfect. When I take a look at a piece that I can tell has been made well, I get a real sense of satisfaction.

For me, I'm the kind of guy that likes to feel he's making something that's—well, how should I put it—something that you can tell requires workmanship.

b) Fair Wages, Job Security, and Bonus. Ninety-nine per cent of the employees describe their wages as "usually excellent, although because of the recession, they are now a little slow" and "could be better, but this is not a complaint just a natural desire for more." The fact that the company does not have a history of layoffs especially during the depression is appreciated deeply by the employees (92 per cent). The bonus at the end of the year is also a feature very prominent in the view of the employees (92 per cent). The employees in A list "steady work, secure job, good wages, bonus" as the second important aspect they like best about the company.

c) Fair Incentive System. Almost all the employees studied are on individual piece-rate system. The rates for the jobs are viewed by the employees as fair. Of all the employees responding to the question about the fairness of the rates only 6 per cent say the rates are not fair. The remainder describe them either as, "They're O.K. I wish they were higher but then who wouldn't.

That's natural," or, "some are tough, some are easy, the over-all average is O.K."

The process by which rates are set is an interesting one. It reflects the attitude of management toward pressure. There are not any motion and time studies made. When a new job comes along the manager and the relevant superintendent meet and decide what is a fair rate. They may call in the foreman and even the employee if they are in doubt. According to the foremen, when their opinion is asked it is usually taken seriously, although the foremen expect a few pennies to be cut off their estimates. The foremen are aware of this practice and add a few extra pennies to the estimated cost. Once a rate is set, it is never changed even if it should turn out to be too loose. Rates are changed only through method changes.

Most of the employees describe the piece rates as fair. At the same time 100 per cent admit that "pushing to make money" is the biggest cause for poor quality work. The piece-rate system forces a man to emphasize quantity more than the quality. Although the highly skilled employees dislike the emphasis on quantity, they admit that they can see why "the company must do this if they are to stay in business" (74 per cent).

For example:

I think the biggest problem with quality is a man doesn't have enough time to do the job the way they should do it. Many of the guys are interested in doing a good job, but they can't.

What happens? Well, the guys get to the point that they don't care about putting out the best product. What they really care about is making the buck. Then, you can't damn the company for saying quantity is important. How in the hell are they going to stay in business.

d) *The "Kitty."* In most cases all the employees interviewed are able to build up a "kitty." Some jobs are timed so that one can earn a lot of money in one day if he produces to the utmost of his assumed capabilities. However, as is the case in many plants, the employees restrict their reported production.[13] They do

---

[13] See William F. Whyte's *Money and Motivation* (New York: Harper & Bros., 1955).

this by simply holding back "tickets" which they must turn in if they are to get paid. The ticket states how much the man produced on a particular item, the piece rate, the order number, etc. Thus if a man produces more than he feels (and in many cases their foremen feel) is wise to turn in, he "banks" the surplus tickets in his "kitty" and holds them until a day when he may be assigned a tough job or when he may not be feeling well or when his machine may break down.

Ninety-seven per cent of the employees report that the "kitty" is very important to them. It provides them a measure of control over their wage fluctuations and helps to guarantee them a steady take-home pay. The remaining 3 per cent feel the same but add they do not make enough.

A kitty is damn important, and you put that down. If you're sick or have a rough day it helps you out. You can take it easy when you're not feeling too well, and still turn in and get paid a good piece rate. I think it's very important. With some jobs, you can't make a kitty. With others you can. Sometimes you get a job that's really rough. You know it and the foreman does too. So, you go ahead and lose and make it up by the kitty. A good foreman makes sure you get an easy job to make up for your loss.

(Same as above and) . . . Of course there is a limit set to the kitty, and I think this is true in all departments. In most departments a limit is set as to how much work you can turn in every day. The foremen tell us it doesn't make sense to turn in all the work. It might upset things.

. . . I don't have to kid you. You know all the departments are told by the foreman, if they really have a good day, not to turn too much money in because the office will wonder.

Exactly how much an employee keeps in his "kitty" is a carefully guarded secret. Some employees who have suddenly quit or have unexpectedly and temporarily been laid off have turned in as much as $400 worth of tickets. This is probably atypical. The range of estimates from the employees on the average "kitty," range from a few days to three weeks. The reason that the amount is kept a secret is *not* fear of management. The fear the employee has is that another employee might learn the size of his "kitty," and if high, feel free to pressure him to turn over to him an easy job.

e) Minimum Pressure from Management. The employees in subsystem A report that there is minimum pressure from management. Thus, 74 per cent report "management in this place is excellent." "They're wonderful people." "They hardly ever bother us, and we hardly ever see them." One hundred per cent respond that the pressure from the leadership and the controls is at a minimum. One hundred per cent report they are their own boss on the job. The only pressure they really sense is during the rush season. The employees report the thing they like best about the entire company is that the management is "friendly," "not chicken," and "does not pressure the employees." Some quantitative examples are:

Management is good. They're not like the ones in many other plants. These people are human. They're down to earth. The thing I like best about them is that they do their best to keep us working, and they leave us alone.

That's what I like about this company. The bosses are good people.

INTERVIEWER: Good people?

Yeah, good people—they're wonderful. We hardly ever see them. They leave us alone. Fine people.

Those skilled employees that see their world as being composed of the characteristics above seem to be highly satisfied. There are a few employees, however, who are not completely satisfied. They tend to report pressure from the incentive system, management, and poor working conditions. These variables leading to dissatisfaction (of a minority) of the employees are represented in the top left and bottom left of Figure 2.

f) Poor Blower System and Lack of Smoking Facilities. About 18 per cent of the employees complain that the blower systems and smoking areas are not adequate. The potency of this complaint is judged to be low not only because 18 per cent of the employees reported it but because of those 18 per cent, only 6 per cent report it is the thing they like least about the company.

g) *Self-Inflicted Pressure through Incentive System.* About 39 per cent of the employees made comments during the interview that related to their feeling that an incentive system creates internal pressure to keep the individual producing. Although there was some dissatisfaction due to the internal pressure, all but one respondent added that they prefer the incentive system to any other method of payment.

These are relevant variables of the high-skilled subsystem. Before we are ready to discuss their impact upon the total system, we need to turn our attention to the low-skilled subsystem.

The Formal Requirements of Subsystem B

a) *Nonchallenging Work.* Eighty-five per cent of the employees report they are performing work that requires minimal abilities and offers little or no challenge. Eighty-seven per cent view their work as "routine," "boring," "dull," and "noninteresting." Some qualitative examples are:

Well, it depends what you mean by satisfaction (silence). As far as I can see, it's a job. If you get a good day's pay, that's what counts. There isn't any other kind of satisfaction that a person can get.

(Laughs) The only satisfaction I get out of this job, Mister, is that I get paid well.

If the work is all right then I make money, and that's my biggest satisfaction. If I don't, I get pissed off. What else is there to be satisfied about? I learned long ago the only thing you can get out of a good job is good pay.

The only reason I work is to make more money. No other reason. Some guys (damn few) say they work for pleasure. They must be bats. How the hell am I supposed to get satisfaction from my job? I'd just as soon go out and dig holes, at least I'd be in the fresh air.

The only satisfaction I get is once in a while. I argue with my boss, and he finally admits I'm right. That really makes me feel good.

b) *Fair Wages, Job Security, and Bonus.* Eighty-one per cent of the employees report their wages are "usually excellent although because of the recession they are now a little slow," and "could be better, but this is simply a natural desire." As in the case of A, the lack of layoffs is deeply appreciated (97 per cent). "Steady work, secure job, good wages and bonus" is the feature the employees in B like best about the organization.

c) *Fair Incentive System.* The employees in subsystem B have basically the same incentive plan as do those in A. Sixty-eight per cent believe the rates are fair. Unlike the employees in A, only 10 per cent view the incentive system as a cause of poor-quality work. The difference is understandable because in B the employees work on semiautomatic machines where their role is primarily one of feeding the machine the raw product. They are not responsible for poor quality; the machine is to be blamed. The employees do blame management for not having a clear standard of quality for the poor quality (43 per cent). The remainder blame the people in other departments.

d) *The "Kitty."* The discussion of the nature and functions of the "kitty" in A applies equally for B. The attitudes toward the "kitty" are also the same. Eighty per cent of the employees believe the "kitty" is "very important" for them, and they wished they could have a larger one (13 per cent refused to comment).

e) *Minimum Pressure from Management.* The management practice of minimum pressure apparently is also to be found in B. Thus 71 per cent of the employees describe the management as "excellent." "They hardly ever bother us." Ninety per cent report no pressure except during the rush season. Eighty-three per cent report they are their own boss on the job.

f) *Poor Blower System and Lack of Smoking Facilities.* Thirty-nine per cent of the employees in B complain about the lack of proper smoking facilities and the poor blower systems. Only 10 per cent of these place this complaint in the category of the thing they like least about the company.

g) *Self-Inflicted Pressure through Incentive System.* Forty-three per cent of the employees comment that the incentive induces self-inflicted pressure. As in the case of A almost all desire the piece-rate system.

The Organizational Predispositions

If we analyze the tables of predispositions described in the previous section, one will find that the four most important predispositions of the employees in A and B are similar. They are the predisposition for wages and job security, noninvolvement, control, and togetherness. These needs "fit" both subsystems well. The management applies little pressure on the employees. It does not require that the employees become highly involved in the formal controls. In fact, up until recently, it had few formal controls such as budgets. Also the management, through its intake process, emphasized that it wants friendly employees who get along with each other and who do not complain. Togetherness is congruent with this requirement.

A fundamental assumption of an effective individual piece-rate incentive system is that the employees will be predisposed to make money and desire secure jobs and will not be greatly influenced by informal group standards. The emphasis on money and job security is mirrored in the predispositions of the employees. Togetherness prevents any cohesive group from forming that creates group standards. The rate-setting in this organization is primarily controlled by the employees' classic fear of overproduction. The foremen share these fears and actively but unofficially set ceilings to production. They restrict the employees in the amount of work that they may report in a given day. The usual figure is not more than twenty-five dollars a day.

However, the employees in A and B also differ significantly in three predispositions. These can be related to the nature of the technology. In the case of the highly skilled system, the predispositions of "high-quality work," "variety," and "generalist" are very important. In the low-skilled system *none* of these needs appear as being important for three fourths of the employees. Rather, in subsystem B, "aloneness," "passivity," and "routineness" or "sameness" are very important. In short high- and low-skill employees develop predispositions that are congruent to the requirements of the technology in their respective subsystems.

The reader may inquire how do we really know the employees developed these needs to conform to the formal requirements *after* they entered the system? Is it not possible that the individuals had these needs before they entered the system? These are crucial questions and to be answered adequately they require longitudinal studies of employees which begin before they enter the labor market and which continue for the working lives of the employees. Thus, at this time conclusive replies cannot be given.

However, there are a few indirect indications to support the hypothesis that the employees in this plant develop the predispositions in accordance with the work world in which they exist. First are the comments made by the employees in B during the discussions about personal satisfactions. Nearly 65 per cent give responses from which the interviewer can infer the respondent is aware of the existence of more mature needs. Many employees (over 50 per cent) made comments such as, "Are you kidding, Doc, what kind of challenges are there in these jobs. Any dodo can do them."

The second bit of evidence is that the highly skilled employees manifest a higher proportion of mature predispositions while the low-skilled employees manifest a much higher proportion of immature needs. If the predispositions were not a function of the work world, then would it not be valid to expect a more normal curve of distribution of predisposition within each subsystem? [14]

The Informal Employee Culture

From research on personality we may hypothesize that individuals will tend to try to guarantee the expression of those predispositions that are important for them. From research on culture we may hypothesize that one way individuals can guarantee the expression of their needs is to create a culture that sanctions and approves these needs.[15]

Although we cannot show the actual mechanism by which it occurs, we hypothesize that this is what happens in Plant X. The

[14] An analysis of available data shows that there are no significant differences between high- and low-skill employees in terms of education, intelligence, age, and ethnic background.

[15] This is not an unwarranted hypothesis. Two of the basic assumptions of the research described as "personality-in-culture" is that (1) the individual and the culture interpenetrate one another and (2) the culture mirrors and provides a basis of sanction for the crucial needs of the individuals in our society. The work of Bakke, Erikson, Kluckhohn, Lewin, Linton, Newcomb, and Sullivan are some examples of scientists whose work supports the hypotheses.

employees in both subsystems create an "informal employee culture" which sanctions *those predispositions that are common to their subsystems*. These are control, wages, job security, noninvolvement, and togetherness. The informal employee culture (IEC) serves as a system to guarantee through cultural norms that the individual needs are maintained in time, which in turn supports the employees in their striving for self-actualization within the plant social system.

Outputs of the Informal Employee Culture

As is pointed out in Chapter I, the pyramid-shaped organization is a strategy of organization based on power and specialization. In an industrial organization management has power over the employees. The employees therefore live in a world where their opportunity for expression of their predispositions would be immediately cut off if the management decided to violate or even throw out the norms of IEC. However, we know from the policies and practices of the company that top management is willing to reinforce the norms of the employee culture. Thus the probability that management would take such action against the culture is small.

High self-expression, in turn, leads the employees to behave in ways desired by management. It is as if the employees say, "Since management is respecting our self-actualization, we will respect theirs." Consequently, the people in Plant X have a high production rate (in the eyes of the management), are loyal employees, show low turnover rates, low grievance rate, and low upward mobility. With regards to low upward mobility it is interesting to note that management, in its official pronouncements, encourages self-development and upward mobility. The employees who see actually very few possibilities for upward mobility view the official pronouncements as necessary propaganda. They believe that management is actually quite grateful that too many employees do not want to better their position. During the feedback session, management confirmed this belief when they responded to the finding of low desire for upward mobility with the attitude, "Well, that's fine. What'll we do with all those people if they want to go up. We'd have a lot of frustrated gripers in our plant and the employees could rightly blame us."

Satisfied Management

Data available show that most of the top management is highly satisfied with the outputs of the informal employee culture. For example, two of the top corporate officers interviewed rate Plant X as "the best" and three rate it as "one of the two best." All independently agree that morale is very high and that the supervision is much above average for the entire corporation.

Turning to the top five officials of the plant, we find that they believe the employees are the best producers in the corporation. They are so confident of their employees' motivation to produce that in response to the question, "How can this plant be made more efficient?" they reply, "By changes in methods, machinery, etc." "If the plant is inefficient," states one, "it is due to not having enough work for him, or the production runs are too short, or our methods are inadequate."

Indices such as turnover, absenteeism, and grievances are so low that formal records are kept other than by the foremen. Excessive scrap and waste does not exist; stealing, gambling, breaking of rules, late attendance, refusals to work overtime on short notice hardly ever occur.

Management's reaction toward the employees is quite positive. During their visits with the employees they express their satisfaction with the employee group. Moreover during their own planning meetings of future changes, the top-line management is especially vocal that the employee culture should not be violated. If it is, one stands the chance of, to quote one line executive, "rocking the boat" and "upsetting the applecart."

Since over the years the employees experience no or very few attempts by management to violate their culture, they infer that it is accepted by management. Thus we have a state of management-employee satisfaction. This may be hypothesized to induce the management "to strengthen" the hiring process and to support the induction of employees similar to those already hired.

We may also hypothesize that this state of "mutual satisfaction" feeds back to reinforce the major predispositions in the employee world. We pause to point out that this provides a self-maintaining subsystem. Here is an example of how the output-input model influences the analysis.

Since the management accepts their predispositions and their culture, the employees feel free to express little interest in knowing about the objectives and other aspects of the formal organization. It is as if they are saying, "Management leaves our informal world alone, we will leave their formal world alone." Thus, over 91 per cent of the employees report they have no suggestions as to how to better their jobs. In the answers to both questions, the employees make it clear that these aspects of the system are not their concern. As one put it, "Look, Doc, we've got a damn good management. That's their worry. This is their company. If they want to tell me anything, or make job changes, they will."

Passive Foreman Leadership

Let us now turn to the foremen all of whom have "come up from the ranks." This immediately implies that the foremen have had their personalities influenced by the informal employee culture.

When made foremen, they are told by managemet that they will be considered successful to the extent that they maintain high production, low turnover, grievance rate, and absenteeism. The foremen realize that the way to get the employees to behave in this manner is to maintain the informal employee culture and not to behave in a way that violates the culture's norms. Thus, 87 per cent of the foremen report that in order to be effective, they must strive hard (1) to keep everyone busy with work that (2) guarantees a fair take-home pay, (3) to distribute the easy and tough jobs fairly, and (4) to leave the employees alone as much as possible. In short, a successful foreman, from the foremen's point of view is neither directive nor is he the expert in human relations that some imply he ought to be. The employees agree with this logic. Eighty-seven per cent in A *and* B describe an "understanding" foreman in terms similar to those above. Some illustrative comments from the employees are:

A man you can trust. He's got to be good for the company and good for the men. He shouldn't bend backwards and get himself kicked in the ass, and he shouldn't screw the men either—do you know what I mean?

Well, I have some definite ideas on that. I think a good foreman is a fellow who works for the company but also for the men. He gives these men a fair shake.

INTERVIEWER: Could you help me understand what you mean by fair shake?

RESPONDENT: Well, I don't mean now that he should bend backwards, in fact if you ask me, he shouldn't bend at all. No sir, not at all. You can't bend backwards here, because they'll walk all over you. What I mean if the men are in trouble and can't get their job done in the way they'd like, he should go over and help the man without getting upset about it.

Well, it's pretty tough to satisfy people around here. You got the human element, with the people on one side, and then you've got the management on the other. And it's not so difficult to satisfy management because they'll tell you exactly what the hell they want, and they make it very clear. But the employees, that's really different. You have to be diplomatic with them, and you've gotta be firm, and you've got to be fair. And how you're going to do this, I don't know. They make requests and some of their requests go clearly against company policies. And yet, you've got to go ahead with some of them because if you don't, they wouldn't co-operate with you.

I like to have a foreman who is understanding. A man who can reason with the help. Not a guy who will fly off the handle, just at any question you ask him. He listens to you and he doesn't have to agree, but he doesn't say to you, "If you don't like it, the hell with it." For example, the other day I wanted something, and the foreman said to me, "I can't do it, if you want to make that change, talk to the superintendent." Now what kind of a foreman is he? It seems to me if he is a foreman, he should talk to the superintendent.

Outputs of a Successful Passive Leadership

We hypothesize two resultants from the passive or "understanding" foreman leadership styles. First is an employee-management relationship dominated by something we shall call the "psychological work contract." Second, a foreman who as a human being and as a leader becomes "simplified."

a) *Psychological Work Contract.* Since the foremen realize the employees in this system will tend to produce optimally under passive leadership, and since the employees agree, a relationship may be hypothesized to evolve between the employees and the foremen which might be called the "psychological work contract." [16] The employee will maintain the high production, low grievances, etc., if the foremen guarantee and respect the norms of the employee informal culture (i.e., let the employees alone, make certain they make adequate wages, and have secure jobs). This is precisely what the employees need. Thus, the foremen's leadership behavior feeds back to guarantee the perpetuation of the employees' predispositions and their informal employee culture.

b) *Simplified Foremen Leadership.* The impact of the psychological contract is to coerce the foremen to mold their leadership pattern in terms of its requirements. But, the requirements are not particularly difficult. They do not require any particular skill from the foremen. All they have to do is leave the employees alone and make certain that they get a fair day's pay. The latter responsibility lies actually with production control and the top management.

In other words, the foremen have very few requirements that might challenge them. Certainly, they do not require complex human relations skills as self-awareness, sensitivity, etc. The psychological contract simplifies the employee-foreman relationship. It also simplifies the foreman's leadership pattern and thus simplifies him as a human being.

In line with this analysis, we find that only 26 per cent of the foremen feel that getting along with people is important. More important perhaps is that only 13 per cent feel they have any ability to get along with people. Sixty-six per cent describe them-

---

[16] The concept "psychological contract" is one created in order to help organize and explain certain phenomena. At this stage, we provide only indirect evidence of its existence. In Chapter V more direct evidence is provided.

selves as "I have nothing to offer except the technical abilities I learned on my job" and "I do not have any abilities; there's not much to me!"

It is not difficult to see why the foremen's predispositions with one exception are similar to those found to exist for employees in B. If the foremen do not feel their work is challenging then they will tend to have similar reactions as to the employees in subsystem B. Thus their predispositions are: (1) not to become involved, (2) to be left alone, and (3) togetherness (for them it is called "understanding").

The foremen also express strong predispositions to have work that contains variety and to be directive. One may hypothesize the internal tensions of people whose predispositions are to be directive but who consciously accept a passive leadership role. One can also begin to understand why few foremen express the need to develop themselves.

Dissatisfied Management with Foremen

A simplified leader does not tend to possess the active, striving, characteristics desired by management. The foreman tends to be quiet passive in his relationship with top management. If it is possible, he prefers (unknowingly at times) to get top management to make any decisions that are important.

Resultants of a Dissatisfied Management

a) *Pressure on the Foremen*. Management reacts to the passive leadership by applying pressure on the foremen to make them, as one top executive said, "more alive, go-getting, and hard-hitting." The foremen feel the pressure. Although few employees report pressure from management, 94 per cent of the foremen report such pressure. Moreover, 77 per cent report that they are never, or hardly ever, their own boss.

b) *Employee Visits*. Because the executives also do not trust the capabilities of the foremen they constantly make visits throughout the plant. There is hardly a moment when the top plant executives are not walking through their respective departments. They tend to be friendly and chat with the employees. As one top executive put it, "I get an accurate feel for the morale of the employees with these visits, and I get it much quicker than it would come to me from the foremen."

These visits are deeply appreciated by the employees. Eighty-seven per cent report that they appreciate the visits from the top management because they report it makes them feel that they are "needed," "appreciated," "important," and "understood." For example:

I think it's a wonderful thing. It gives people a big boost. If a person of higher standing walks through and is willing to put himself more on your level, and you're a lower-standing person, then you feel like really helping him. What the hell do you feel with a man who knows he has higher standing, and wants you to know it. You really don't like him, he's stuck-up. This is what I like about so many of our top people. They go around and they don't act like they're God. They act like they are one of us.

Well, as they say in Texas, it's downright friendly. Seems to me when a supervisor or manager does come around, stops at the desk, and says hello, how's the family—you get a good feeling. A feeling that they're on your side.

INTERVIEWER: When you say they're on your side, could you help me understand that?

RESPONDENT: Well, this is my own opinion, I don't know how other people think. But it seems to me that if the top brass is out, the people feel that the top brass is out here to pay you as little as they can and get as much work as they can from you. This you expect from any manager. That's his job. Now if the top brass creates a feeling that if they're on the employees' side, then at least this—you don't get the feeling that they are going to screw you.

A careful analysis of these visits, however, points up the fact that none of the executives spend more than sixty to ninety seconds with each employee. One reason that the visits are so short is that management does not want to prevent the employee from producing the output to which he is aspiring. Another is, "There is really not much to say." The question that comes to mind is what is the psychological state of these employees that they feel it is logical to be appreciated, feel deeply understood by, and close to, a management with whom they have apparently skin-surface, fleeting contacts? How can an employee contend that he feels truly understood and appreciated if he literally experiences "passing" contact with the manager? These are questions which, at the moment, must remain unanswered. However, they may provide some interesting hypotheses about mental health in organizations.

Another reason why employees enjoy fleeting contacts may be related to the employee's emotional concern about the fact that he is relatively helpless and under the control of the manager. It can be quite reassuring to interact with a manager who comes to tell you he wants to be friendly. A friendly manager is not as threatening; he probably would not consider acting arbitrarily in relation to the employee.

Many employees express that they feel some tension when they first note that a top manager is walking toward them or is bending over them apparently to say hello. Until something is said there is always the probability that something is wrong. Once the employees realize the manager means simply to be friendly their tension is reduced and they are greatly relieved.

There is a cultural dimension to this problem that also requires consideration. In this plant (as in most industrial plants) there is in operation a company policy which is called "management by exception." The basic assumption is that an organization should develop accurate information about its production activities. The actual production level should be compared with a projected production level which management, through careful study, adopts as the optimum production level. If the studies are accurate then the actual rate should not vary significantly from the optimum rate. If the actual is much higher or lower, something is assumed to be wrong. It is at this point that management goes into action.

The point is that action is taken when production deviates from the expected level. When there is an "exception" to the prediction then action is required. In most industrial plants, this "principle" may have permeated most types of control activity (waste, errors, inventory, etc.). Thus it has important effects upon the interaction of individuals. It is understandable why an individual may hypothesize that a budget man will not usually visit a production man; a foreman, the employee; a superintendent, the general foremen; a quality control expert, the line production manager, etc., unless something is wrong. As one man put it, "Our boss hardly ever bothers us. In fact he tells us, 'Don't worry if I don't talk to you. That means you are doing well. It's when I come looking for you that you should worry.'"

It may be, therefore, that a norm develops in an organization that "no interaction" is "good interaction." In stating the hypotheses we do *not* imply that there are not many interactions among people in industry for reasons other than coping with difficulties. We are simply suggesting that one factor that may influence any given individual's feelings about his boss is the "principle by exception" which tends to permeate most industrial organizations. It helps to provide another reason why the employee may tend to feel greatly relieved when he sees his boss approach him to hear, "Hello Joe, just stopped to see how things are going and to say a friendly hello."

If we may hypothesize that the visits may act to assure the employee that management "still loves him," then the employee may also conclude that management approves of him as a person, the informal employee culture and the psychological work contrast. In the language of system analysis, management's visits feed back to reinforce the system of accepted predisposition, the employee informal culture and the psychological work contract. Again we find another feedback loop that reinforces the hiring process, and we see another mechanism that tends the system toward equilibrium and self-maintenance.

The Foreman's Job: Low Status; Undercutting; and Decision Carriers

If the management's visits act to increase the employee satisfaction, they tend to increase the foremen's dissatisfaction. Many feel that they are undercut (77 per cent). They feel they are not truly trusted; that their job is menial with not much responsibility. Sixty per cent describe their work as "completely routine," "dull," "nonchallenging," or "routine with variety once in awhile."

This attitude about the foreman's status also exists for the employees. For example:

Who me, be a foreman? Are you kidding? What the hell do those guys do? They're not foremen, they're lackies.

INTERVIEWER: Lackies?

RESPONDENT: Yeah, whatever they say upstairs the foremen do. For example, if a foreman sets a price, he tells us that he will set it a little loose because he will have to fight his boss. Now you figure that out. You're part of management, and you have to fight them.

No, I don't want to be a foreman. First of all, I don't believe that they're really real foremen. They don't make the decisions, somebody else does. These guys are, I don't know how else to put it, they're just like a jackass. You know, you whip it, and you tell it what to do, and that's what they do. On top of that, there's not enough money. But even if they gave me all the money I wanted, I wouldn't take that kind of job.

Foremen Dissatisfaction

We can now state that the foremen's dissatisfaction is primarily influenced by at least four factors. They are the pressure from the management, low status of their job, undercutting, and their role as decision carriers rather than decision makers. A fifth important factor is the low wages in relation to the employees' wages. A little over half of the foremen earn less than the average of their department. Clearly, this is an example of lack of status congruence (i.e., the discrepancy between one's pay and one's formal position) which has been shown to lead to dissatisfaction.[17] However, in this case the lack of status congruence cannot by any means explain the totality of the foremen dissatisfaction. Nearly one third of the foremen are highly satisfied with their wages yet all but one of these have extremely low morale and feel quite bitter. If the lack of status congruence is a crucial variable then one would expect a greater number of the foremen who report they receive high wages and are satisfied with their pay to also express relatively high morale. Moreover the lower wages paid

---

[17] See for example the recent work of Professor George Homans.

to the foremen does not represent a completely unfair position on the part of the management because the foremen have a number of benefits not available to employees (e.g., guarantee wages even though work is seasonal, extra insurance, and sick benefits, and larger retirement benefits). Finally, we shall see (Chapter VI) that in another plant (Plant Y) where the foremen are paid much better wages relative to Plant X foremen and to their own employees, the foremen's morale is even worse than it is in Plant X.

The Resultants of the Foremen's Dissatisfactions

a) *A Desire for More Money.*   The foremen being passive do not feel free to communicate their complaints to the top management directly. The theory predicts that one way to express their complaints is to desire much higher wages than they are presently receiving. The logic is the greater the dissatisfaction, the greater the emphasis on money. Thus, although employees in A and B do *not* express a predisposition for higher wages (in the sense that the present ones are unfair), 64 per cent of the foremen manifest such a predisposition. This result is unfortunately not as conclusive as we would like because influencing it is the fact that the foremen perceive their wages as being low in the first place. At the same time, the low wages act to entrench the foremen even further in the passive leadership role. This in turn acts to increase management's reaction in the direction described above. We now have a closed circuit resulting in foremen and management dissatisfaction each behaving in such a way to increase the other's dissatisfaction.

b) *A Desire for Higher Status.*   Seventy-seven per cent of the foremen express a wish that management would do something to raise the status of the foremen's job.

c) *A Desire for Greater Control.*   Seventy-seven per cent of the foremen make statements to the effect that they wish the top-management pressure would decrease and that they would be given more control over their job.

d) *Reinforcement of the Simplified Personality.*   The dissatisfaction also feeds back to reinforce, in the minds of the foremen, that they best remain dependent as they are and not become ego-involved in the company's formal problems. Such an attitude leads to a few foremen desiring self-development.

Reinforcement of Management Dissatisfaction with the Foremen

The resultants of the foremen's dissatisfaction by no means pleases management. They feel that the foremen are not facing reality if they think that the best way to adapt to their (management's) pressure is to become even more "simplified," dependent, and submissive while at the same time asking for higher control. Thus the foremen's adaptive activities reinforces the management's feelings of dissatisfaction which only serves to increase the management's pressure, employee visits, etc. The "management-foremen" circuit is now closed, and we have another self-maintaining feedback process. This leaves the management with the employees as their major source of satisfaction, which in turn feeds back to reinforce the particular hiring process now being used (which management views as highly responsible for the type of employee now working at Plant X). This feedback completes the circuit to the input process, and we have still another self-maintaining feedback process.

CHAPTER

IV

The Usefulness of the Organitional Analysis to the Resear

THERE ARE at least two tests of the usefulness of the model of organization that has just been presented. One is the extent which it serves to deepen one's understanding of the organization, especially of variables that are different from those already obtained. The second, and a resultant of the first, is the new predictions that one is able to infer from the model which subsequently are verified.

In this chapter four examples of the usefulness of the framework are presented. The first is an example of the deepening of our understanding of the organization. The other three are examples of concrete predictions about future human behavior in the organization that are independent of this analysis.

Quantifying the Individual's Degree of Self-Actualization

One of the central problems of organizational theory is the understanding of the individual's self-actualization within the organization.[1] One major stumbling block is the difficulty of ascertaining what precisely does an individual desire to actualize while at work? It has been the belief that trying to ascertain the predispositions of individuals is too complex a problem especially

---

[1] Recently the writer has noted the work of Blum who seems to be one of the few trying to systematically quantify the individual's *and* the organization's actualization. See for example, F. Blum, "Social Audit of Enterprise," *Harvard Business Review,* Vol. XXXVI, No. 2 (March), pp. 77–86.

for large numbers of cases. It is thought, on the assumption of individual differences, that the number of predispositions for example, would be unmanageable. Compounding the problem is the one of depth. How "deep" does one delve into the individual personality to understand it in order to make valid predictions?

Beginning with the former problem there are a number of forces acting to decrease the heterogeneity of human predispositions within an organization. First, the very function of organizational structure, managerial controls, leadership, job descriptions, policies, and practices is to require psychologically different people to behave in remarkably similar ways. For example, ten supervisors who can be shown to have different personality patterns (on the basis of projective tests) may behave similarly when they are in the plant manager's office.[2] In another example researchers have shown that the assembly line (or other types of technology) coerce psychologically different employees to behave in similar manner.[3] It is results such as that which may help to provide insight into why the total number of different predispositions found to exist in a bank (300 employees), a hospital (250 employees), and in this manufacturing plant (400 employees) does not exceed twenty.[4]

Turning to the problem of depth one must differentiate between those who find opportunity while at work to express large portions of their personality (usually management) from those who do not usually obtain optimal self-actualization (the lower-level employees). In the case of the lower-level employees, as is suggested in this study, such a narrow range of their personality is expressed while at work that one does not have to go very much in depth to understand their behavior relevant to *the organization setting*. However, when one interviews executives who work in a world characterized by interpersonal relationships that in-

---

[2] Chris Argyris, *Executive Leadership* (New York: Harper & Bros., 1953). For a systematic discussion of this phenomenon see the discussion of "behavioral settings" by Roger G. Barker, and Herbert Wright, *Midwest* (Evanston: Row, Peterson & Co., 1954).

[3] See the work of the Technology Project at Yale University and Professor Leonard Sayles' at Columbia.

[4] The socio-cultural matrix may also act in the same direction.

volve their whole personalities, deeper studies may be necessary if a full understanding is to be obtained.

Knowing the predispositions of individuals is only half the task. One must also know the demands that the organization makes upon the individuals in order to compute the probable degree of expression the individual will obtain.[5] The model presented in the previous chapter which purports to include the relevant demands of the total organization upon the individual serves the purpose. (Relevant for understanding self-actualization.) Combining the system of ascertaining personality predispositions with the model of the system presented in the previous chapter, it is possible to ascertain and to quantify although crudely the degree of self-actualization of any given employee on any level.[6]

The first step toward this quantification is to define a scale of the degree of self-actualization. We hypothesize that the individual's perceived degree of self-actualization, with the organization will be:

0. *Zero* when that individual reports (or when we can infer that he perceives) no expression of his personality requirements;
1. *Minimal* when the individual reports (or when he can infer that he perceives) that he is obtaining some personality expression but that it is not adequate.
2. *Adequate* when the individual reports (or when we can infer that he perceives) that he is obtaining adequate personality expression;
3. *Maximum* when the individual reports (or when he can infer that he perceives) that he is obtaining as much personality expression as he desires.

Constructing the Individual's Self-Actualizing Score

In order to arrive at an individual's self-actualization score each interview is analyzed and scored as follows:

---

[5] For an excellent study of personality assessment where the environmental demands are systematically understood see, George G. Stern, Morris J. Stein, and Benjamin S. Bloos, *Methods in Personality Assessment* (Glencoe, Ill.: Free Press, 1956).

[6] It is also possible to ascertain and quantify the degree to which the organization actualizes itself. The quantification process of the organization's actualization is not yet adequately developed and will not be discussed in this volume.

1. Analyzing the interviews; list all the predispositions that the individual reports (or the researcher infers) he desires to express.
2. To the right of each predisposition list the reported (or inferred) degree of expression of the factor using the scale above as the guide. This may be called the "Actual Expression." (*AE*)
3. Multiply each *AE* score by the potency that the predisposition has for the individual. Regular = 1; very high = 2; and extremely high = 4. (*AE* × *P*)
4. Total the column of (*AE* × *P*) scores.
5. Then list the maximum possible score of each predisposition which in all cases is 3. (*ME*)
6. Multiply this score by the potency. (*ME* × *P*)
7. Total the (*ME* × *P*) column.
8. Then place the result of (*AE* × *P*) over the results obtained by (*ME* × *P*).

The number obtained is simply a score. It serves to place the individual in a position on a scale ranging from zero to one. If A has a score of .60 and B has a score of .30, all we may say is that A's score is higher; but we may not say that A's score is twice as high as B's.

An example of a typical work sheet would be:

Predispositions	AE	P	AE × P	ME	ME × P
Control	2	2	4	3	6
Togetherness	3	2	6	3	6
Noninvolvement	3	4	12	3	12
Direct	2	1	2	3	3
Wages	2	1	2	3	3
High-quality work	2	1	2	3	3
			28		33

$$\frac{(AE \times P)}{(ME \times P)} \quad \frac{28}{33} \quad \begin{array}{r} .848 = .85 \\ \overline{)28.000} \\ \underline{264} \\ 160 \\ \underline{132} \\ 280 \end{array}$$

The scales described in the paper admit only to ordinal properties. Thus the numbers 0, 1, 2, 3 are meant to mean nothing more than that 1 is larger than 0, 2 is larger than 1, and 3 is larger than 2. Nothing is said about *how* much larger one is from the other. The zero point is defined as that point where the individual reports absolutely no expression of the factor being considered.

Having made these comments, it behooves us to admit that if we use the term "ordinal scale" in its rigorous meaning, then we have no right to add and multiply the numbers in order to arrive at the self-actualizing score. In order to multiply and add we must have scales with cardinal properties.

There are available mathematical gymnastics to overcome this problem.[7] However, they were not available to the writer when the first phase of the research was conducted. The interesting fact however is that the resulting scores do work in that they have a respectable degree of predictive validity. The only defense that comes to mind regarding this "sin" (that seems to work) is that, "if one is not willing, temporarily at least, to 'sin bravely' (but explicitly and self-consciously) against the best canons of scientific technique, one should face up to the fact that progress . . . is for the time being out of the question." [8]

A few further words about the procedures just described. Much of their validity depends upon the frame of reference and the subjective judgment of the researcher. This makes replication by another researcher difficult and consequently decreases the probability to which the method can become "public."

The writer is aware of the problem and is striving to correct the situation. One possible approach is to discard the present dimensions and study dimensions that are more easily quantified. However, in the writer's experience he has never been able to quantify in rigorous terms, the variables that seem most relevant to him (given the theoretical framework). He tends to reject the notion that it is best to quantify rigorously and study variables that admittedly are not as relevant as those which cannot be quantified rigorously.

One of the reasons for the resistance is frankly an emotional

---

[7] I am indebted to Dr. James Marsh (Carnegie Institute of Technology) for bringing this point to my attention.

[8] Marion J. Levy, "Some Aspects of 'Structural-Functional' Analysis and Political Science" in Ronald Young (ed.), *Approaches to the Study of Politics* (Evanston, Ill.: Northwestern University Press, 1958), pp. 59–60.

one. If one deeply feels he is "junking" that which is most crucial to him, then his sense of personal "inner congruence" is not very high. This researcher pleads guilty to the fact that he has never been satisfied with dimensions simply because they scale neatly.

Another reason for the resistance is related to the concept of rigorousness and to one's aspiration as to how long it will take to achieve the desired state of rigorousness. Let us explore the latter point first. One cannot object to social scientists setting for themselves high standards for research. It makes sense to aspire to relatively objective and therefore publicly verifiable measuring instruments. But is it useful to be critical of less rigorous methods (which however admittedly tap relevant variables) because they have not achieved the standards ultimately desired? Isn't there some room for the possibility that it will take much time before those studying human behavior in organization may emulate their physical science colleagues (if they should be emulated)? The writer tends to find the physical scientist much more supportive of slow movement and emphasis on the qualitative insights during the early stages of scientific development. In fact a number of them (especially mathematicians) tend to become impatient when they read about social scientists trying to use methods that are not appropriate to the level of development of their research. This is the position Robert Oppenheimer takes in the article cited in Chapter I. He lauds, for example, the insightful and highly qualitative work of Piaget.

In making the plea for the respect of qualitative insights during the early stages of development, one does not deny the importance of the ultimate objective. It is precisely because he wishes to reach it that one asks for patience. The goal after all is *not* objectivity and rigorousness *per se;* it is objectivity and rigorousness *with the variables that are relevant*. True rigorousness therefore is related to dealing with relevant variables and the relevant complexity.

The behavioral scientist in dealing with the problem of rigorousness with complexity may find it useful to turn to the medical researcher. He too aspires to the development of objective research and diagnostic instruments. However, he is not free to select for the study those variables or that aspect of the problem that is easily quantifiable. He must, above all, study those variables that are hypothesized to be relevant even if they are complex.

It is interesting to observe the humility with which medical researchers approach the problem of contructing publicly verifiable measuring instruments. The writer has observed a research seminar on the interpretation of X-rays attended by specialists in radiology. Medical researchers with a minimum of eight years of medical training and practice, having available fine photographic equipment and ingenious diagnostic techniques, have great difficulty in diagnosing "a little black spot." One soon learns that medical researchers know, namely that "the little black spot" that looks objective is by no means that objective. In fact there is a pooling of judgments and a final decision is made only after hours of discussion. Yet, with the complex phenomena facing the behavioral scientist, the researcher in most graduate schools is admonished to develop "objective" measuring instruments that another (usually disinterested) graduate student can without any (if possible) or little (if necessary) training replicate the measurements obtained by the researcher who has spent many months, if not years, on the project. Is this not being quite presumptious!

This leads to another related hypothesis. Speaking of the area of interest in this book, the contruction of instruments that are independent of the researcher may be premature. In fact, it may be that the study of such variables as conflict, frustration, defenses, etc., is best accomplished in a relationship where the research instruments will always include the "living-in-relationship" with the subject referred to in Chapter I.

Briefly, we suggest that instead of attempting to separate the researcher from the subject, the opposite direction is suggested. The researcher-subject relationship is a human one. It must be studied with great care in order to make explicit what is "in" the researcher that facilitates or inhibits data collection. Once we learn that, then we may be able to teach it to others. Admittedly this implies that the researcher may be asked to modify his interpersonal behavior. It might be a good thing from a society's point of view to ask behavioral scientists to become more aware of themselves and their impact upon others.[9] It may help to insure that those of us who are interested in research (partly) for power reasons will at least be aware of this as part of our motivational structure. Such public awareness may well be part of the control system that the society may have to impose on the researcher as his research becomes more powerful and as his services are increasingly desired.

The Self-Actualizing Scores

From the discussion in the previous chapter one might conclude that the self-actualizing scores will be high. This is confirmed by the examination of the frequency distribution of the scores (Table 4).

TABLE 4

FREQUENCY DISTRIBUTION OF SELF-ACTUALIZATION
SCORES IN SUBSYSTEM A AND B
In Per Cent

	Dept. A	Dept. B
0–49.5		
50–54.5	2.9	1.1
55–59.5	2.9	1.1
60–64.5		3.3
65–69.5	5.9	8.9
70–74.5	5.9	16.7
75–79.5	8.8	11.1
80–84.5	23.6	16.7
85–89.5	20.6	21.1
90–94.5	14.7	10.0
95–100	8.8	10.0

The Operational Validity of the Actual Expression Scores

An important question that must be asked is how do we know that the degree of expression (AE) assigned to each predisposition is valid? In order to test the validity of the actual expression scores a random sample of 25 interviews was given to two pro-

---

[9] Note: Nothing is said about requiring behavioral scientists to change their behavior.

fessional social scientists. They were asked to study the model of the social system (given in the previous chapter). They were asked to make a judgment as to the actual degree of expression of the predispositions in each interview. The judges were in agreement with each other in 69 per cent of the cases. The agreement between each judge and the writer was 73 per cent and 76 per cent respectively. These data lead us to conclude that the operational validity of the scales used above may be adequate.

The Predictive Validity of the Self-Actualizing Scores

It would increase the value of the self-actualizing scores if something can be predicted from them that is independent of the data gathered up to this point. Self-actualizing scores would then have predictive validity. In two other organizational studies where the turnover was high the scores were used to predict who would and who would not leave the organization on their own motivation.[10] The results in those two organizations indicated the scores had a high predictive validity. Such a test is not strictly possible in this study because the turnover is almost nonexistent. The low turnover would certainly be predicted on the basis of the scores provided in Table 5 above. In this sense, the predictive validity is high. However, for a rigorous test the scores should be subjected to a test situation where there is a high turnover rate. This would provide ample opportunity for the scores to fail if they were not valid.

Another possible value of the self-actualizing scores has been evolving from some very preliminary work being conducted by the writer. Let us assume that the higher the self-actualizing the more productive (in Fromm's sense) and mentally healthy is an individual. By borrowing some concepts from the field of medical epidemiology the self-actualizing scores might form the basis for understanding how mental illness or health and human productiveness are spread throughout the organization being studied.

For example, let us focus on four employees who work together. They are found to have self-actualizing scores of 30, 60, 75, and 90 respectively. The individual with a score of 90 enjoys

---

[10] See the bank and hospital studies by the author.

a deep sense of satisfaction; the one with a score of 30 is highly frustrated. This individual can be conceptualized as a "carrier" of tension, frustration, and dissatisfaction. We will assume that a "host" to a given carrier (Mr. 30) will be the person with the closest score to Mr. 30. This is Mr. 60. Indeed, we find by actual observation that Mr. 30 interacts more with Mr. 60 than with anyone else.

Mr. 30, the carrier, contacts Mr. 60, the host, and is able to transmit the "disease" of tension and dissatisfaction to Mr. 60. Unlike the yellow-fever mosquito that dies when he infects a host, Mr. 30 has his "disease" of dissatisfaction reinforced from the success experience of infecting Mr. 60.

By our definition Mr. 75 is a host to tension and dissatisfaction from Mr. 60 who now has become a carrier. Again, empirical evidence confirms our assumption. Mr. 75 said in an interview, "That jerk (Mr. 30) is always complaining, but Joe (Mr. 60) hardly ever complains. I have to think twice when I listen to him." If Mr. 60 succeeds in infecting Mr. 75, then Mr. 75 may infect Mr. 90, who is the host for Mr. 75. In the process of spreading the "disease" each carrier has his "disease" reinforced when he sees that his attempts at infection have succeeded. The reinforcement of the disease may be represented quantitatively by a decrease in the self-actualizing scores.[11]

The above is presented primarily as an illustration of the possible research directions of the self-actualizing scores. Why would it not be possible to obtain self-actualizing scores on all human beings in organization and on the basis of interaction patterns (and/or sociograms) predict the spread of "illness" or "health," depending on whether the carriers are spreading human satisfaction or dissatisfaction. Such an analysis could help one to discover the actual processes by which one department, one plant, or even a community becomes ill, while another seems to develop increasing health. None of these questions can be answered at

---

[11] I am indebted to Dr. Warren Bennis from M.I.T. for pointing out that the analogy has difficulties because it may be that an unhappy or infected person may infect a happy person to feel even better. One would have to spell out under what conditions one obtained positive or negative contagion.

this time. Much research is needed before the empirical validity of this projected approach can be ascertained.

Predictions Regarding the Impact of Change

From the model in the previous chapter we concluded that the employees' behavior is guided primarily by the informal employee culture and the psychological work contract.

If these conclusions are valid, then the following hypotheses may be stated:

a) Since the predisposition of wages and job security is an important one for the employees, they will tend to accept organizational changes as long as the changes do not decrease their wages and job security.

b) Since the predisposition of noninvolvement is an important one for the employees, they will tend to accept change *without* desiring to participate in the planning of these changes.

c) Since the predisposition for control is an important one for the employees, they will *initially* be annoyed with changes in their work but this annoyance should decrease as the employees gain control over the new job.

An opportunity to test these hypotheses arose in one of the high-skill departments. In this department the employees produce "total" products primarily by hand. The level of skill is among the highest in the industry.

The management decided to mechanize the production of a particular product in order to cut the costs and hopefully the price. From our interviews we learned that almost no opportunity was given to the employees to participate in planning the change. It was simply announced to them that such a change was being planned. Nothing else was communicated to the employees until the new work process was developed and ready to be installed. At that time the men were shown the new process, a lecture was given to them, and a short demonstration made. The new process required so little skill, that relatively untrained female employees could perform the work with little training. Thus the change is a very significant one in terms of the decrease of skill required.

On the basis of our analysis any resistance to change should be due to fear of job security, a decrease in wages, or loss of control and not due to such factors as lack of participation and involvement in the change process.

The results were as predicted. Ninety-three per cent of the employees reported initial fear of loss of wages.[12] These fears were quickly overcome because management had purposely set loose piece rates so that the men could earn their accustomed wages or more with little effort and even during the learning period. However, the fear of job insecurity increased somewhat because the employees now felt with more of the product on the market (even at a lower price) they were at the mercy of the sales department even more than before.

During the interviews 83 per cent of the employees responded that they did not care that they were not included in the planning of the changes. "That is management's worry," commented one employee. Moreover, 92 per cent of the employees viewed the changes as necessary if the company is to remain in a good competitive position.

The only complaint mentioned by the employees was that the quality of the product was reduced by the new semiautomatic process. Fifty-five per cent decried the de-emphasis of quality work. This complaint is also predictable from knowing that employees in A are predisposed to high-quality work.

Finally, an unexpected finding on the basis of previous studies (but not unexpected from the model of Plant X) *none* of the employees complained about the fact that their jobs had been "de-skilled." The interviews show that the employees do *not* feel their original jobs are de-skilled. They view that the company is simply paying them these wages to perform different work.

An illustrative comment is:

I think management introduced the merry-go-round (the nickname given to the new process) correctly. There's no need in calling the people in and wasting a hell of a lot of time. You tell them what you plan to do, you guarantee their pay, you guarantee their job security, and then you let them think about it. When you're ready you put it in. Sure they complain a little bit, but it's quieted down now.

---

[12] $N = 30$.

Management's Reaction to the Feedback

Another situation which can be used to test the predictive validity of the organizational diagnosis made in the previous chapter is the feedback sessions. If the analysis is valid, then specific predictions can be made about the probable reaction of the management to the feedback data.

The following hypotheses were stated before but tested *during* the feedback session.

Hypothesis A. Since, according to our model, the management tends to view the capabilities of the foremen with doubt and since they feel they must pressure the foremen, they will not be surprised by the feedback of information that implies the foremen feel under pressure and have a number of complaints regarding the low status of their job.

Hypothesis B. Since the management tends to view their relationship with the employees as satisfying they will tend to be surprised when the employees' predispositions of noninvolvement, control, aloneness are mentioned.

Evidence for Hypotheses A and B. An analysis of a tape recording of the first and second feedback sessions confirm the two hypotheses. All four managers express surprise at the apathy and noninvolvement of the employees. They also stated that the results about the foremen were as expected. Identical results were obtained during the feedback session with the corporate management (12 present).

Hypothesis C. Since the management tend to be dissatisfied with the foreman and satisfied with the employees, they will tend to consider only recommendations that require changes of the foremen and their informal culture.

Evidence for Hypothesis C. An analysis of the tape recording of the plant feedback shows that during the discussion about the analysis six suggestions were made by the management for changes and all were related to the foremen.

The specific content of most of the suggestions was also hypothesized to be as follows:

Hypothesis D. Since management emphasizes material rewards, and since they view the incentive system as the best type of material reward, they will tend to make suggestions about how to improve the foreman situation in terms of raising wages (perhaps through an incentive system) and at the same time raising the standards for the foremen.

Evidence for Hypothesis D. Four of the six suggestions were concerned with raising the wages of the foremen and expecting more of them. The researcher was also told that the management was seriously considering an incentive system for the foremen. Four of the six suggestions were also related to giving the foremen a "human relations" training course.

The Impact of Change on the Total System

In Chapter I we state that organizations are a pattern of variables tending toward stability. Since the model represented in the previous chapter purports to conceptualize an organization, then it follows that it must tend toward stability. It can be hypothesized therefore that any changes designed to significantly alter any of the variables presented in the model or their position will tend to be resisted by the system.

A change that implies basic alterations of the system has just been introduced into the organization. It began about the time when half of the employees had been interviewed. The change is the introduction of a budget system to more rigorous control costs.

The philosophy and impact of budget requires (according to the people in the controller's office) that they apply never-ending pressure (1) to raise continually production goals and (2) to cut freedom for error, (3) to tighten increasingly the piece-rate systems, and (4) to strive to eliminate informal activities such as the kitty.[13]

Since this philosophy is held by the budget people in this or-

---

[13] For a general discussion on the impact of budgets see, Chris Argyris, and Frank Miller, under the direction of Schuyler Dean Hoslett, *The Impact of Budgets on People* (Controllership Foundation, 1951).

ganization, then the system will be pressured by the budgets to change. More specifically the management will be forced to increase its interaction with, and pressure on, the foremen to "tighten up." Should this behavior occur it will only serve to increase the foremen's discontent, desire for money, and feelings of second-class citizenship.

The foremen, we predict, should resist passing the pressure down to the employees. Budgets violate the psychological contract. Pressure, increased interaction, tightening up on piece rates, and elimination of the kitty would lead to dramatic changes in the system. The foreman, recognizing this possibility will tend to resist budgets.

But, since the pressure emanates from management and since they are expected to be loyal to management, it will be difficult for the foremen to resist openly.

We may further predict that management's *low* evaluation of the competence of the foremen will tend to delay the effective operation of the new budget system thereby making the change *easier* for the people. Thus the foremen can complain that the budget system is too complex and consequently, it will require much time to be introduced. The management, in turn, perceiving the foremen as not being particularly bright will tend to accept these excuses and lower their level of aspiration as to the time the change will require.

Unfortunately because of the recency of the introduction of the budgeting process not enough data are available to systematically test these predictions. However, the data that are available support the analysis.[14]

Interviews with the three top-management personnel clearly bring out the foremen's complaints regarding the complexity of budgeting. The managers report that this is expected since as one put it, "our foremen have never had budgets and of course they're not so bright." On the other hand, observations of two budget sessions show that the foremen *are* being pressured. They counteract with silence, with careful digs at the budget system and excuses for not meeting the goals.

---

[14] In the next chapter some of these hypotheses are tested more rigorously.

In interviews with four of the foremen (two of whom are perceived by management as being weak), they report that the foremen are having difficulty with budgets, but they do not feel they should report their difficulties to top management. The foremen also report that they fear what will happen if the employees see their budgets as pressure devices. As one put it:

Jessuz, I can't use these goddam things as the bright boys upstairs think they can be used. Why if I take one of these damn things to the boys in Department A, most of whom have been in this company over ten years, they'd tell me to shove them.

Another said:

It's easy for them guys to talk about modern methods of control. But, have they ever tried to put these things across to people who never had to use budgets and who have been lead by bosses who wouldn't give a good damn for budgets? I wonder what the hell will happen as the pressure grows. And it will.

Interviews with the budget control people leave little doubt that they believe that Plant X can be tightened up much more. The top budget people express disgust with the length of time it is taking to really use budgets as they wish. As one put it, "Someday someone is going to have to light a fire cracker under somebody's rear. All we hear is excuses and all we get are delays. Look here, take a look at these figures. . . ."

Although the data above indicate a trend congruent with the one hypothesized above, it is still too early to present systematic evidence. The data above are presented to lend support to the suggestion that the model can be used to predict the impact that budgets will tend to have on the system.

It is hoped that these four examples illustrate the view that the diagnostic model is able to help in deepening the understanding of the organization. It can also help to make valid predictions about events that may occur (e.g., change) and those that will occur at a future time (e.g., the first feedback sessions were conducted three months after the definition of the hypothesis).

CHAPTER

V

Predicting the Impact of Organizational Changes in Plant Y

WE HAVE shown how a model may be constructed that helps us to understand aspects of human behavior in a given organization. The fruits of understanding are prediction and control. Control exists when the researcher, at his own desire, and by his own plan and action, manipulates what he is studying. The ultimate in control is to create that phenomena which one is studying.

Control is difficult to achieve when one studies actual organizations because of the complexity of the phenomena and the fact that the researcher cannot easily manipulate an organization. The organizational researcher is closer to the position of the meteorologist and the scientist studying high altitude cosmic rays. In both cases the state of knowledge is so underdeveloped and the phenomena are so difficult to control that one is pleased if by successive approximations he is able to hypothesize what precisely will occur under specific conditions and then wait (in the case of the meteorologist) or send up his balloon (in the case of the cosmic ray student) hoping that the conditions he has hypothesized will in fact occur.

Prediction, therefore, may be one major fruit of understanding that can be offered at this time to develop the theoretical point of view.

There are however several kinds of predictions that one can

120

make. One of these, upon which we focus, may be called naturalistic prediction. Bales defines natural prediction as the "prediction of natural events" (e.g., weather). He admits that such predictions are most difficult because of the large number of relevant
and interrelated (and therefore difficult to control) variables.
Nevertheless, he continues, in spite of the complexity, naturalistic
prediction is the "next" goal that social science research must consider if it is to maintain an exacting criterion of scientific progress.

Bales provides clues into the characteristic of "naturalistic
prediction" when he discusses the use of such predictions in the
"interpersonal arts." Naturalistic predictions require that one is
able to diagnose accurately what is going on, predict where it is
going, and how it will change if he (or any one else) takes a given
action—and to do this early enough for interventions to be possible should it be deemed desirable.[1]

It follows that the second phase of the research ought to emphasize the stating and testing of a priori hypotheses inferred
from the model used to understand Plant X. How may this be
achieved? One possibility that immediately comes to mind is to
conduct research in Plant X on the impact of the changes brought
on by the increased use of managerial controls such as budgeting. This possibility is rejected because these changes have just
begun and not enough time has elapsed in order for the changes
to have had an impact upon the organization that our relatively
primitive research instruments could measure with a respectable
degree of accuracy.[2]

Another possibility is to locate a plant (e.g., Plant Y) whose
social system until recently was similar to that of Plant X and
which is presently experiencing a "tightening-up" process
through the increased use of new managerial controls. On the
basis of the model of Plant X it should then be possible to derive
hypotheses and make specific predictions as to what the researcher will find in Plant Y. If we know that a "tightening-up"

---

[1] Robert T. Bales, "Small-Group Theory and Research" in R. K. Merton,
L. Broom, and L. S. Cattrell, Jr. (eds.), *Sociology Today* (New York: Basic
Books, Inc., 1959), pp. 294–97.

[2] Recent interviews with management of Plant X suggest that the predictions confirmed in Plant Y are now also valid for Plant X.

process is going on in a particular plant (Y), and if the social system of Y is similar to X, then we should be able to predict where in the system of Y the changes will occur. Also, we should be able to predict the direction and hopefully the amount of change that will occur within the social system of Plant Y.

To state it in more operational terms, we should predict on the basis of the Plant X model, the content of the responses to be found in Plant Y to the questions (Chapter II) and the probable percentages that we would find for each (or sets of) variable(s).

In order to conduct such a study it would be necessary for Plant Y to be located within the same culture, the same corporate structure, and to have a similar technology, organizational structure, leadership, managerial controls, etc. Also, it should have been undergoing the tightening-up process for a long enough period of time that predictions might be tested.

Such an opportunity was found to exist in Plant Y which is part of the corporation presently being studied. Plant Y's technology is similar to Plant X and has had the budgetary and other "tightening-up" changes introduced earlier than Plant X. Would management permit a study of Plant Y?

The answer was provided in a rather interesting manner. The reader may recall that Plant X was considered by management as one of their "outstanding" plants. The feedback of the research data, however, raised questions in their own minds about their evaluations (and about our conclusions). As part of a series of steps designed to resolve these questions they concluded that the next step would be to study a plant which in their own mind was not as "healthy" as Plant X. They asked the research group, therefore, to study Plant Y.

As soon as permission was received to study Plant Y some refinements were introduced in the research design. It was felt that in addition to the objective of predicting how Plant Y will differ from Plant X, it would be more interesting if a priori predictions could be made about differences *within* Plant Y. Would it be possible for example, to predict those departments within Plant Y that will tend to have higher and those that will tend to have lower morale; higher absenteeism, lower absenteeism; higher interest in the quality of their work, lower interest in quality, etc.

For the purposes of comparison, the management of Plant Y was also asked to state their predictions regarding the differences in morale, etc., among the departments within the plant. The management of Plant Y selected two departments that they felt had "high morale" and two that had low morale. Fifty per cent of the employees in each department ($N = 15$) were interviewed. All the managerial personnel ($N = 25$) were interviewed and some observed by the use of nonparticipant observation. The total number of employees interviewed therefore is 60 and the total number of managers is 25.

Ascertaining the Degree of Congruence between the Social System of Plant X and Y

Before stating a priori hypotheses about Plant Y's social system and its differences from Plant X, it is necessary to present evidence that the model of Plant X's social system is valid for Plant Y.

What is meant by "valid?" In assuming that the Plant X model is valid, we are assuming (1) the variables that are relevant for Plant X are relevant for Y and (2) the *patterning* of the variables (their *position* in the model) is not different. We do *not* state that different values may not exist for each variable. Thus the percentages for such variables as "fair wages," "nonchallenging work," "excellent kitty," "challenging work," etc., may differ between Plant X and Y. It is the objective of the research to predict a priori what these differences will be. The research should also make explicit why and how these differences between X and Y arose and continue to exist, and to define hypotheses about their future state.

Turning to the evidence that the variables relevant in the Plant X model are also relevant for Y, we first note that the personnel function is centralized and therefore the same people and the same policies and practices constitute the hiring process in Plant Y.

Both plants have a high-skill subsystem (A) and a low-skill subsystem (B) into which the employees may enter. Two of the

four departments selected for intensive study are low skill and
two are high-skill departments. Incidentally in the eyes of management the two low-skill departments (La and Lb) have low

TABLE 5

COMPARISON OF VALUES OF THE VARIABLES
IN SUBSYSTEM A IN PLANTS X AND Y
Expressed in Per Cent

	Plant X (N = 34)	Plant Y (N = 30)	Stat. Sig.
1. Challenging work.................83		76	
a) Many abilities required..........83		76	
b) Plenty of variety................88		90	
2. Fair wages, job security.............99		93	
3. Bonus...........................92		100	
4. Fair incentive system...............94		90	
5. The "kitty".......................97		96	
6. Poor blower system, etc............18		70	.0001*

* The "*p*-values" are given for those figures that are statistically significant.
In the body of the text the *p*-values are given at the end of the appropriate sentence.

The probability of obtaining by chance a difference as large as that reported is
computed by employing statistical procedures appropriate for use with independent
proportions. See Quinn McNemar, *Psychological Statistics* (New York: John Wiley
& Sons, Inc., 1955), p. 60. I wish to thank Robert Fromer for his help in the statistical analysis.

TABLE 6

COMPARISON OF THE VALUES OF VARIABLES
IN SUBSYSTEM B IN PLANT X AND Y
Expressed in Per Cent

	Plant X (N = 90)	Plant Y (N = 30)	Stat. Sig.
1. Nonchallenging work			
a) None or minimal abilities required..85		84	
b) No variety; no challenge.........85		83	
2. Fair wages and job security.........81		80	
3. Bonus............................97		100	
4. Fair incentive system...............68		60	
5. The "kitty".......................80		90	
6. Poor blower system.................39		53	.0110

morale and the two high-skill departments (Ha and Hb) have
high morale.[3]

---

[3] The management's diagnoses does not turn out to be a completely valid
one. The reasons will be discussed later on.

In Tables 5 and 6 summaries are presented of the percentages of each variable in subsystems A and B in Plant X and Y.

Let us first examine subsystem A in both plants. We note that the identical variables are found to exist in both plants. The values of the variables challenging work, fair wages and job security, bonus, fair incentive system and the kitty are *not* (statistically) significantly different. There are some differences and they will be discussed in the next section since they illustrate the hypotheses to be tested.[4]

Turning to subsystem B in Plant X and Y, we note again that the identical variables are found to exist in both plants. The values of the variables, nonchallenging work, fair wages, job security, bonus, fair incentive system, and the kitty are not significantly different.

The expected similarities are also found when we analyze the predispositions. The most important predispositions mentioned in *both* plants in subsystem A are control, wages, and job security, noninvolvement, togetherness, high-quality work, variety, and generalist. The only significant difference is that in Plant X 51 per cent of the men report a need to be directive while 33 per cent report the same need in Plant Y (.0110). Data are not available to explain the discrepancy. One possibility is that the difference may be accounted for by the fact that one of the highly skilled departments in Plant Y has a high proportion of older employees who are near retirement and tend to prefer a more passive role in the organization.

In subsystem B we find the most important predispositions mentioned in *both* plants are wages and job security, noninvolvement, togetherness, control, aloneness, passiveness, and routine. The only significant difference noted is that 90 per cent of the employees in Plant X need aloneness while only 70 per cent report the same need in Plant Y (.0002).

Finally, as in Plant X, the four major predispositions for *both*

[4] The values differ significantly for "poor blower systems, etc." Actually Plant Y is a relatively new plant which in the eyes of the employees has apparently been poorly designed. The blowers, according to the employees, do not function effectively and the lighting is installed too high.

subsystems are fair wages, control, noninvolvement, and togetherness.[5]

The Process of Stating a Priori Hypotheses about What the Researchers Will Find in Plant Y

The only information the writer had about Plant Y *before* conducting the research was that a general "tightening-up" process
had been instituted in the plant about one year ago. The aims of
the "tightening-up" were, and still are (1) to cut costs, (2) to
develop accurate cost standards, and (3) accurate inventory control. Generally speaking, costs were to be cut by reducing wherever feasible the costs of production work. Errors, waste, and
poor quality are especially to be reduced.

With this knowledge, the writer returned to the university and
set before him the analysis of Plant X (Chapter III and IV plus
Figure 2) and began to define any hypothesis that came to mind.
Some of the kinds of questions in the writer's mind that influenced the direction of his thinking were as follows:

Where (in Plant Y) will management apply the pressure for
reduced costs? How will subsystems A and B (Plant Y) tend to
react to the tightening-up processes? What will be the impact of
the pressure on the low- and high-skill employees, the foremen,
the informal employee culture, the psychological contract, etc.?
How will the foremen tend to react? How will the employees' and
foremen's reactions tend to affect the other parts of the social system?

Fifteen a priori hypotheses were derived from these logical ex-
ercises. Ten were related to the impact of change upon the employees and five to the impact of the change upon the foremen.
These fifteen hypotheses were placed in an envelope and were not
referred to until the time came to write the results (about one
year later). Although the writer did not look at the hypotheses
during the year, the fact that he stated the hypotheses, conducted

---

[5] The reader may question if the similarity in variables found is not really
due to the fact that the same questions were used in both plants. It is assumed
that with the other open-ended questions used during the interview the respondents have an opportunity to include whatever variables are important to them.

the interviews, and analyzed the data raises a question as to the degree to which the knowledge of the hypotheses consciously (or unconsciously) influenced his interviewing activities and the subsequent analyses of the interviews. This is a limitation of the research project. It would have been better to have someone independent of the research project to derive the hypotheses or to conduct the empirical research. Although such action would seem to be desirable, the one used in the present analysis can with appropriate controls provide adequate validity.

The first question that may be raised is how do we know that the hypotheses stated actually came from theoretical framework and the model and not from the experiences of the writer in Plant X. One way to test this question would be to ask some scholars who have no connection with the project to derive whatever hypotheses they feel they can on the basis of the theory and data available up to this point. Two such scholars were asked to perform this activity independently of one another. In both cases after three hours of discussion about the theory and method the scholars were able to derive all the hypotheses that the writer had derived. Naturally, the two scholars were not told of the writer's predictions. The reader may wish to "test" these results by attempting to derive his own hypotheses because he now has before him most of the data the writer used during his analysis.

An even more difficult question is to what extent the knowledge of the hypotheses influenced the researcher in his interviewing behavior and his analysis of the data. Before dealing with this question it may be useful to point out that even without stating the hypotheses explicitly the researcher could not help but be influenced by the previous year's research. Therefore, making the hypotheses explicit *before* the research begins at least helps the researcher to be more aware when he may be trying to influence the situation so that the data may come out as he hypothesized.

There is another reason why stating the hypotheses a priori may not necessarily be harmful when one is conducting field research. The researcher conducting organizational research is fully aware of the primitiveness of his theory. He is also aware that the few hypotheses he is able to state a priori will by no means cover the full range of data that will be discovered during the research project. Thus if he knowingly distorts his data to accommodate a few hypotheses, he runs the risk of not being able to account for other data which are frequently uncovered during the research. The probability of this occurring is by no means small. The a priori hypotheses defined actually "covered" only a little over a half of the data obtained.

Perhaps the most important evidence available that knowledge of the hypotheses did not unduly influence the researcher is the fact that several hypotheses are tested by data that are obtained independently of the interview situation and the researcher. For example, predictions about turnover, absenteeism, quality of work, and errors in work are tested by data collected by the organization and not by the researcher. All but one of these hypotheses was confirmed by data obtained directly from management records.

Another possibility to be considered is that the writer was unknowingly (unconsciously) influenced by the process of a priori stating the hypotheses. If these influences were unconscious then they presumably would be beyond his control. If these influences were beyond his control, then one might hypothesize that they ought to distribute themselves evenly throughout all the interviews. For example, if an unconscious bias exists within the researcher to confirm his prediction that Plant Y will tend to report more pressure than Plant X, then the bias should be distributed evenly in all the interviews. But as the reader will see shortly there are departments within Plant Y that report little pressure while others (in line with the hypothesis) report much pressure.

The reader may also ask if it is not logical to assume that the writer was biased unconsciously by the management ratings of low morale and high morale which were available to him before he began the research. The answer seems to be negative because the results obtained contradict the management predictions (more about this later).

Still another question is if the researcher became biased during each interview as he listened to the replies. Thus when the employees reported that their kitty was taken away from them, he would immediately predict greater pressure, and thereby become "contaminated" for the remainder of the interviews. There are really two replies involved. First, not all employees reported resentment when their kitty was taken away. In fact nearly one half of the employees in two departments reported the opposite conclusion. Second, even if the above were not the case, the bias being considered would influence *any* researcher who was aware and had intellectually internalized the theoretical framework being used. These biases are impossible to erase. In fact would it not be incorrect to try to erase them? A researcher guided by a theoretical viewpoint does not have an unbiased view. Any theory is a bias about what is and what is not relevant. Thus, if such biases operated during the research, they would be expected and desired since these are the biases one is trying to test.

One comment about the presentation of the hypotheses. Those hypotheses that are a priori are numbered with Roman numerals. At least ten hypotheses were defined *after* much of the data were collected to account for results not predicted at the outset. The writer wishes to point out that because the a priori hypotheses form the outline for the presentation that follows, *no* implication is made that they are considered to be more important than the hypotheses derived after the data had been collected.

Hypotheses about the Impact of the Changes upon the Foremen in Plant Y

We hypothesize that since "pressure activities" are already an integral part of the management-foremen relationship (see Figure 2, pages 82–83) and since the employee-management relationship does not contain pressure activities, the management will tend to place a higher degree of pressure upon the foremen than upon the employees.

The reader may suggest that such a hypothesis can be derived from general knowledge about management activities with any formal organization. Any management group will tend to put pressure on the lower-level management during such changes. This argument would be a valid one if this is all we are hypothesizing. But we are implying more.

We note that the existing management-employee relationships, although relatively skin-surfaced, are reported as being satisfying to most of the employees in Plant X and Y. Management will tend to find it embarrassing to bring pressure into these relationships. This is unusual because in many plants top management does not hesitate to personally institute cost reduction campaigns (through plant speeches, poster campaigns, prizes, etc.) in order that the employees realize that they are not only instituting the changes, they are supporting them enthusiastically. To the writer's knowledge, this did not occur in Plant X or Y.

Let us now turn to the a priori hypotheses that we stated about the impact of the change upon the foremen.

Hypothesis I: Plant Y Foremen Will Report Greater Pressure than Plant X Foremen. Since the foremen in Plant X describe the changes as "pressuring them" and since the same changes have been introduced at Plant Y for a longer time period at an increased pace, we hypothesize that the foremen in Plant Y should report a greater degree of pressure upon them than do the foremen in Plant X.

Evidence for Hypothesis I. The responses to the specific question dealing with pressure do not clearly confirm the hypothesis. Ninety-three per cent of the foremen in Plant X and only 88 per cent in Y report they experience pressure ($N = 30$ in Plant X and $N = 25$ in Plant Y).

A detailed examination, however, of other related evidence leads one to conclude that the figures above represent the number of foremen who report pressure but *not* the *intensity* of the pressure. The intensity may be indicated in a number of ways. First, we note that only 77 per cent in Plant X desire higher status to get away from being pressured whereas 92 per cent request the same in Plant Y. Moreover, whereas 63 per cent (in Plant X) of these assign it a "high potency." But 76 per cent in Plant Y assign it an "extremely high potency" value whereas none in Plant X assign it the same value (.0001). Another indirect indication is that none of the foremen in Plant X reported "absolutely no satisfactions from my job" whereas 24 per cent of the foremen in Plant Y reported such lack of satisfaction and relate it directly to the pressure that they are experiencing.

I'll tell you if you really want to know the problem of a foreman. I heard a young foreman put it beautifully the other night at one of our functions. He had a couple of beers in him, and he was talking to some of the people in his department. And he said something like this. "Every one of you bastards should be gunning for my job, but none of you bastards, not one goddam of you, wants my job, now do you?—and I don't blame you."

We've had meetings, you know. Well, a while ago we had a meeting at the office, and he told us straight out that by God we had to straighten out or else they are going to make an example out of a few of us. Not one man would speak up, you know why? I'll tell you why, because we're afraid. Everyone of us are afraid. We haven't got the guts to tell those guys why the hell don't they wise up and see what they're doing to us.

Well, I do know that they think of us but only by their actions. Maybe it is beginning to change a little bit, but I'd say a year ago management had a very low regard for us. I had occasion to hear higher ups really bitchin' and call us everything from we're no good to just bastards; they just dragged us up there and they told us that they thought that we were not doing a good job and that by God we have to do a better job. Now I felt that if they really disliked us as much as they were sounding they should have fired all of us. So what do they do all of a sudden, they want better quality, and they feel that all you have to do is snap your fingers and you get better quality. They haven't any idea of the new tools and the material and so on that we need. You don't get the feeling that you're even worse than the workers because in this plant, Mister, there's no question about it, the workers are thought of more highly than is a foreman.

Frankly, sometimes I wish I could tell them to go to hell. They think that we could work harder, honestly, I doubt if I could work any harder. I'm out here breaking my neck. I have never taken an afternoon break. I used to take my work home, and I finally gave it up because I thought that was wrong. If they could just give us a fair reward. But in this company, if you're not a producer you're just dead overhead, just dead overhead. Where the hell can you go?

Well, I don't know. I don't think that they really like us. I think that they feel we're here, they've got us where they want us, and they feel we've got to stay in one place. We feel that they want to hold us down, and that's the thing we feel mostly about them is that they're holding us down; they're keeping us under control. I think they're pretty stern sometimes in the way they express their opinion about us. When they don't really know the whole view. When it was first started, I think the foremen wanted to tell them off, but now of course they're not. Many of them, quite frankly, have said the hell with it. Why should he worry about it, let them worry about the company. I think that's the feeling that most of them have, and that's the feeling I'm beginning to have, and I don't like it! Because I don't think that's right.

Hypothesis II: Plant Y Foremen Will Place Greater Emphasis on Upward Mobility than Plant X Foremen.   Since upward mobility is one adaptive activity open to participants in organizations (see propositions in Chapter I), and since the foremen cannot use such adaptive activities as unionization, apathy, etc. (see propositions in Chapter I), and since the Plant Y foremen report themselves to be more pressured and frustrated than the foremen in Plant X, we predict that they will have a greater desire for upward mobility than do the foremen in Plant X.

Evidence for Hypothesis II.   In presenting the evidence it should be kept in mind that the opportunity for upward promotions are on a company-wide basis. Therefore, the foremen in Plants X and Y have equal opportunity for any openings that might exist.

In Plant X 47 per cent of the foremen actively desire to be promoted whereas 72 per cent actively desire it in Plant Y (.0307).

Hypothesis III: Plant Y Foremen Will Place Greater Emphasis on Money than Plant X Foremen.   Since emphasis on money is one adaptive activity open to participants in organizations (see propositions in Chapter I), and since foremen cannot use such adaptive activities as unionization, apathy, etc., and since the Plant Y foremen report themselves to be more pressured and frustrated than the foremen in Plant X, we predict that they will tend to emphasize the importance of wages more than do the foremen in Plant X.[6]

Evidence for Hypothesis III. Sixty-four per cent of the foremen in Plant X and 92 per cent of the foremen in Plant Y report that they should obtain higher wages (.0075). (The company's figures indicate that the foremen as a group in Plant Y make more money than the foremen in Plant X.)

Foremen wages are very low. Management I'd presume sets a particular rate, and I guess they figure if we don't like it that's tough. But I think the boys feel that it is very low. You might ask how come we are not doing something about it. Well, that's something I've wondered about. I think most of us go to the management about it individually—sometimes I wonder if we shouldn't go as a group. But then that sounds like a union, and I don't think we should have a union in this plant. We've always done very well without a union.

Well, that I can answer very clearly. I think there is a lot of grumbling and the fellows are quite dissatisfied. For example, let's say in a department where the men are making $2.50 an hour, well, a foreman won't make more than $2.25 or $2.40 an hour. I know what you're going to ask me now—why the hell did he take the job? Well, when they approach you for the job, they really know how to sell it, they approach it in the right way. They'll tell you the opportunities are great and the future is pretty bright and that as you go along things will get better, but you know what happens—that never happens. It never really gets better. And I guess they feel that they've got you, and then there's nothing that they have to really do. I've always felt that the least they should do is make the foreman equal to the top man in his department.

Hypothesis IV: Plant Y Will Have Greater Absenteeism and Turnover than Plant X Foremen. Since absenteeism and turnover are two adaptive activities open to participants in organization (see propositions in Chapter I), and since the foremen cannot use such adaptive activities as unionization, apathy, etc., and since the Plant Y foremen report themselves to be more pressured and frustrated than the foremen in Plant X, we predict that they

---

[6] One might question if foremen will not naturally complain about their wages since they are viewed as less than the employees'. Although the point is a valid one, it is not the one being hypothesized. We are testing the predictions that although the foremen in Y make more money than those in X, they will be even more unhappy about their wages than the foremen in X.

will have a higher degree of absenteeism and turnover than do the foremen in Plant X.

Evidence for Hypothesis IV.   The data available do not support the hypothesis regarding turnover. The amount in each plant is insignificant. Some reasons why turnover is low may be found in the reports of the foremen that they feel they (1) are too old to leave, (2) have no other job opportunity available, and (3) have a high investment in the form of benefits which they would lose if they left. Available data support the last two possibilities. The greater majority of the men who report they wish they could leave also report that they dare not because jobs are very difficult to find. A somewhat less number place the reason for not leaving upon the benefits.

Hypothesis V: Foremen Will Not Be Perceived by the Employees as the Cause of Pressure.   If employees in Plant Y report they are pressured, and if the psychological contract is "in force," we predict that they will *not* tend to assign the cause of the pressure to the foremen.

Evidence for Hypothesis V.   Before the evidence is presented it is necessary to show that the concepts of "psychological contract" and "understanding foremen" exist in Plant Y. The evidence obtained suggests that these concepts are very much alive in Plant Y. One hundred per cent of the employees in subsystems A and B (Y) report the importance of this concept. This is a greater emphasis than is found in Plant X (A = 69 per cent and B = 67 per cent). One might conjecture that the importance of being an "understanding foreman" is greater in Plant Y because the organizational pressure and the individual internal tension is greater. Therefore, a greater premium is placed by the employees on being left alone by the foremen. It is significant to note that nearly 30 per cent more employees (in Y) ask that a foreman be "a stable guy" who "bends backwards and doesn't blow his top no matter how badly the employee shoots his mouth off." One may infer that the internal tension is increasing and the individuals find themselves increasingly "blowing their top." They desire a foreman who understands them and does not blow his top.

Hypotheses about the Impact of the Changes upon the Employees

Hypothesis VI: The Major Points of Initial Impact of the Change upon the Employees' World Will Be on (1) the Kitty, (2) Pressure from Management, and (3) the Piece Rates. Since top management's concept of motivating employees is to provide them with high wages, high benefits, and high job security, and since top management has a policy of never changing the rate of a job, we can predict that the major points of initial contact for change in subsystems A and B of Plant Y will be (1) the kitty, (2) the pressure from management, and (3) redefining the jobs so that piece rates may be altered.

Evidence for Hypothesis VI. Since the redefinition of jobs is more or less an obvious prediction which could easily be derived from the general knowledge of industry practices, suffice to say that major changes were made in job design when the employees moved from the old plant into the new one. No new major redefinitions to the writer's knowledge have occurred since.

Turning to the kitty we find abundant evidence that it is one of the first variables which management attempted to change in Plant Y. A policy was defined at the early stages of the change that no one may have more than one day's pay (or about $25) as a kitty. All kitties above that figure were to be turned in and the employees would be reimbursed financially. From that date on all kitties were to be held by the foremen and wherever feasible an IBM system would be installed where the "machine" would keep track of each man's daily production, including his kitty.

Hypothesis VII: The Organizational Tightening-up Processes Will Be Resented by the Employees in Plant Y. Since the kitty is related to the predispositions of control, wages, and job security, and since these are important predispositions for the Plant Y employees, we predict that the reduction of the kitty and the elimination of "job control" by the employees will be resented by the employees. Also, since we know kitties tend to be higher in subsystem A (Plant X), we predict that the resentment will be higher in subsystem A than B (Plant Y).

Before this hypotheses may be tested, we need to establish that

TABLE 7

COMPARISON OF SCORES REGARDING
MINIMUM PRESSURE FROM MANAGEMENT IN PLANT X AND Y
Expressed in Per Cent

	SUBSYSTEM A			SUBSYSTEM B		
	Plant X(N = 34)	Plant Y(N = 30)	Stat. Sig.	Plant X(N = 90)	Plant Y(N = 30)	Stat. Sig.
1. Management lets us alone..............	74	40	.0028	74	46	.0024
2. We are our own boss...............	100	50	>.0001	83	40	>.0001
3. Pressure is at a minimum..........	100	73	.0006	90	77	.0329

they are (1) never their own boss and (2) that the pressure is high.

Table 8 below summarizes the results. All the differences are in the predicted direction and most are statistically significant.

TABLE 8

COMPARISON OF SCORES REGARDING
MAXIMUM PRESSURE FROM MANAGEMENT IN PLANT X AND Y
Expressed in Per Cent

	SUBSYSTEM A			SUBSYSTEM B		
	Plant X(N = 34)	Plant Y(N = 30)	Stat. Sig.	Plant X(N = 90)	Plant Y(N = 30)	Stat. Sig.
1. I am never my own boss...............	0	50	>.0001	17	60	>.0001
2. The pressure is very high...............	0	27	.0006	10	13	(not sig.)

Further supportive evidence is found in the analysis of the questions, "The thing I like least about the Plant Y is. . . ." We find that only 10 per cent in subsystem B of the employees report that they dislike the new pressure most. However, 53 per cent of the employees in subsystem A report that they like the pressure least of all (.0002). The differences are even more impressive if we compare the figures above with those of Plant X. None of the employees in B and none in A report "pressure" as the thing they like least about the company (>.0001).

Finally, another indication that subsystem A employees (in Plant Y) feel more pressured than do subsystem B (Plant Y) is obtained when we note that in B 43 per cent of the employees feel there is little or no pressure now (compared with the day they began to work at Plant X) and 23 per cent report more pressure. On the other hand, no employees in subsystem A report less pressure while 77 per cent report greater pressure ($>.0001$).

The next series of hypotheses was not defined a priori but follows from the analysis above.

Since we have shown that the top management will not tend to personally apply pressure on the employees and since we know the foremen are not perceived as pressure givers by the employees, then we predict:

1. The middle management will be viewed as the culprit by the employees (even though the employees clearly assign the responsibility of initiating the tightening up process to the top management).
2. The degree of hostility toward the middle management will be greatest in subsystem A since we have established that the pressure is greatest there.

To test hypothesis one above, we note that 92 per cent of the employees in A and B report that they do not see the top management often and that the top management is not pressuring the employees. Eight per cent place the source of the pressure on top management ($.0001$).

On the other hand, 52 per cent of the same employees describe the middle-management executives with such statements as, "too dominating," "not stable enough," "too damn easily upset," "confused," and "ready to give hell but not praise" ($>.0001$). Only 4.9 per cent report them as being "fair" and not dominating. The remainder report that they do not know the middle management enough to comment.

To test the second hypothesis, we note that 43 per cent of the employees in B (Y) perceive the middle management as pressuring them while 52 per cent of the employees in A report the same.[7] It is interesting to view these results with the fact that the

---

[7] Almost statistically significant.

majority of the middle management evaluated the two departments in A as having the high morale and the two departments in B as having low morale.

Hypothesis IX: Self-Inflicted Pressure Will Be Greatest in Subsystem A (Plant Y). Since wages and job security are important for the employees, and since their kitty is reduced, we predict that the employees will tend to compensate by striving to "make out" (i.e., make a day's pay) every day. If this is valid, then we would expect a significant increase in "self-inflicted pressure" felt by the employees in subsystem A and B, Plant Y (over that reported by the employees in Plant X), caused by their need to produce enough every day to make "a fair day's pay."

Evidence for Hypothesis IX. The data confirm the hypothesis. In Plant X the self-inflicted pressure to produce and "make out" every day is 39 per cent for A and 43 per cent for B. On the other hand, self-inflicted pressure in Y is reported by 73 per cent in A (.0034) and 87 per cent in B (>.0001).

Hypothesis X: Employees in Plant Y Will Decrease Their Emphasis on Quality Work. Since the employees in Plant Y place greater emphasis on "making out" than do employees in Plant X, we predict that a greater number of Plant Y employees will report that they cannot achieve a high-quality job because they feel pressured to produce quantity in order to make what they feel is a fair day's pay. Moreover, we predict that a greater proportion of employees in A rather than in B (Plant Y) will report they cannot achieve high quality.

Evidence for Hypothesis X. The data confirm the hypothesis. Seventy-one per cent in A (Plant X) and 90 per cent in A (Plant Y) report that they cannot achieve the quality they desire because of the pressure to make money (.0294). Ten per cent in B (Plant X) and 80 per cent in B (Plant Y) report similar responses (>.0001).

Some illustrative qualitative comments are:

If rates are good the man will give to the best of his ability. Now I don't give good quality all the time, Mister. I'll be the first to tell you, I try to give good quality. But, I know past a certain point if I don't wise up I won't make a day's pay. When I know that, then I start punching them out. Most of the help would like to give a good quality job, but they can't. If a man gets the feeling that he's a way behind, he's not going to get too fussy, because if he gets fussy, he may give good quality but his family will starve.

Our job is to set the thing up and see that it works all right, bring out the first couple of pieces and show it to the foreman. If he likes it, then you go ahead. There is a certain amount of tension in piecework, you never know when you're going to make the next day's pay, whether they're going to have enough work for you. You kind of worry about whether you are going to make a day's pay so that if you get a nice long run of stuff, you're willing to try and put out. But, if you get a bad day and a hell of a lot of bad runs or you get something which the piece rates are pretty low or something that isn't coming out right, then you have trouble. Because sometimes they don't want to pay for extra operations. So what do you do, you just say oh well, the hell with this, and you keep on going. You know dog gone well that the quality isn't going to be any good. What else can you do, how else are you going to make a day's pay? It hurts you now to put out bad stuff, but sometimes there's nothing you can do about it.

I don't think they worry about it. I don't think they have any pride in the job. They only have pride in piecework. You know, I can remember myself, years ago I used to look at a piece, and I'd say you know what I'm doing, I'm working on an important piece of goods. Today I look at it and I say, you know what I'm doing, I'm working on 55 cents.

Hypothesis XI: Plant Y Employees Will Not Tend to Feed Back to Management Their Negative Feelings about the Change. Since the employees tend to perceive the foremen as "ineffective" and "second-class citizens," and since they have established no patterned relationships with top management in which hostility is sanctioned, we predict that the employees will not tend to communicate their negative feelings to (1) the foremen, and (2) the members of upper management.

Evidence for Hypothesis XI. 1. Seventy-nine per cent of the employees report their foremen's influence to be "not very much," "inadequate," and "none," "therefore, there isn't much sense in complaining to those guys because they're pushed as it is and they can't do anything anyway." Only 7 per cent view the foremen as having adequate authority ($>.0001$).

2. We have no direct evidence to test the hypothesis regarding communication to top management. This is partially due to the fact that the data exists on a more covert level. However, indirect evidence that confirms the hypothesis is available.

a) During the research project only two employees were observed or reported to have stopped top management and questioned them on the increased pressure whenever the latter made one of their frequent visits.

b) On the basis of their "visits" the managers were asked to predict which departments would have low morale and which would have high morale. The results were interesting. The managers selected the two low-skill departments as having the lower morale because "of generally less work and lower wages." When the employees in these departments were asked to describe their own morale 37 per cent report, "it is high" and 63 per cent report, "it is low." When asked how they judge "low morale," 67 per cent report that low morale exists because of less work and lower wages. Thus, the management's prediction is relatively accurate (although they misjudge nearly one third of the employees' views of their morale).

However, in the two departments they chose as having high morale (again based on wages) 67 per cent of the employees report they have low morale. The employees attribute their low morale to the increased management pressure and the reduction of the kitty.

The point we are making is that management is relatively accurate in its prediction of low morale when it is due to low earnings because this information is communicated upwards by the employees. However, the management is a relatively poor predictor of "high morale" because they again use wages as their criterion and are not aware (nor are they informed by the employees) of the impact of pressure. The management prediction that the employees in the "high morale" departments are satisfied with their wages is confirmed since 93 per cent of the employees report their wages as "very good" or "satisfactory." What management is not aware of is that the criterion for low morale is beginning to be enlarged and that the new criteria will not tend to be communicated to them.

Hypothesis XII: Employees Will Not Tend to Create Cohesive Informal Groups.   Since the predispositions togetherness and noninvolvement are very important to the employees, we predict that they will not tend to develop cohesive groups that can be used to combat management pressure.

Evidence for Hypothesis XII.   Indirect evidence that confirms the hypothesis is found when one asks the employees (especially in subsystem A) why they do not communicate their complaints to top management. Fifty-seven per cent respond that no cohesive groups exist within the plant and that the employees do not trust one another. Forty-two per cent of the remainder state that they, "Could not understand it themselves," or "I wish I knew, funniest damn thing but employees here have never banded together."

Kitty, I'd say is very very important. Everybody wanted it. Now when the fellows heard they weren't going to have a kitty, they didn't like it at all. They didn't like it at all, believe me.

QUESTION: Could you help me to understand if the employees have done anything about it?

ANSWER: Nothing, what can they do about it? They tell you, and that's it. Is there anything else you can do about it? You see most of the men here, they don't stick together. It's a dog-eat-dog world. Everybody's trying to get the best jobs the easiest jobs that pay the most money for the least amount of work. So they're competing one against the other. Well, when you get that kind of situation, you don't get people who'll stick together and work.

Well, I think they're very friendly. We help each other out.

QUESTION: Could you help me understand how friendly they get?

ANSWER: Well, if you mean do they make friends, so that they go out and see each other I don't think too much. You have to be very careful. For example, in my case, I learned long ago that you must not fraternize too much with the employees. Because you go out with one guy and the people are beginning to bitch that you're probably handing him all the easy jobs, so I hardly ever see them. Although, I'm very friendly with them.

Well, there's not the friendly, real friendly feeling at all that we used to have, course, anybody says hello to one another. But you don't really belong any more in the way we used to belong. People are not close-knit.

Not too friendly, I'd say. The way conditions are today—you know, one man is out to get the other. You know for yourself that the almighty buck, that's the important thing. Everybody says hello to one another, if that's what you mean. But really down deep inside I don't think people are particularly friendly.

QUESTION: I wonder what's made this change?

ANSWER: Well, it's hard to say. Today the only thing you really look out for is can you make a buck so that you can buy the things you want. And that's not too much different when you look at what management's doing. What they're asking for is the same thing. Can they make a buck? They've cut down on quality. It's not what it used to be.

Very friendly. You can tell. People say hello to one another, but you know you have to be careful because with all this damn pressure, you're going around and complaining and bitching and it's not good for you. And it's not good for the employees. Just this morning someone said, "Hey, what did you do, swallow your hate pill this morning?" I wasn't aware of that.

It is interesting to point out that the noninvolvement, apathy, and togetherness that the employees sanction as major components of their culture may also act to *prevent* them from communicating upwards the negative reactions of tension, hostility, etc., and prevent them from uniting to combat the pressure that they are beginning to experience. We may hypothesize further that no hostile employee reaction will tend to be taken until cohesive groups are formed. In order to develop cohesive groups, however, major cultural changes will have to take place within the *employee* subsystem. Unfortunately, data are not available to predict what point the individual pressure will stimulate some kind of group reaction.

Stotland's recent study is relevant at this point. He concludes that expression of direct, overt hostility to a threatening power figure tends to occur more frequently when individuals belong to supportive peer groups.[8] Without a supportive peer group the individual tends to accept the power figure more and to attribute more co-operativeness and reasonableness to him than do those individuals who belong to a supportive peer group.

In Plant Y we find that many individual employees report an increase in pressure, which leads to internal tensions. However, none of the individual tension has irradiated to influence the employees as a group. This point provides us with some clues as to why the pressure on individuals can increase radically and yet no organizational disequilibrium be reported. We have an example of an increase in *individual disturbance* while there isn't (as yet) any inferrible *organizational disturbance*. By organizational disequilibrium we shall mean that state of a system (see Figure 2, pages 82–83) where the *position* of any variable in the pattern is altered. The values of a given variable may change but the system will not be upset until the position of any one or combination of variables is changed.

It would be useful to predict by what processes and at what point the individual disturbance will become so great that the position of the variables will change and the system will be upset. It would give us much needed insight into the tolerance of the system for stability and change. Such knowledge might lead to understanding why, when, and how some organizations explode, and why some do not.

Hypothesis XIII: The More Mature Employees in Plant Y Will Tend to (1) *Express a Relatively High Desire for Unionization,* (2) *Be Absent More, and* (3) *Produce Proportionally More with Less Quality.* Since the theoretical scheme (see propositions in Chapter I) defines the informal behavior as adaptive behavior, and since the necessity of adaptation is greatest where the frustration is greatest, and since the pressure will act to make the employees more dependent, submissive, etc., we predict that the more mature employees (in terms of our model) will be the most

---

[8] Ezra Stotland, "Peer Groups and Reactions to Power Figures," D. Cartwright (ed.), *Studies in Social Power* (Ann Arbor: University of Michigan, 1959), pp. 66–67.

frustrated. Moreover, on the basis of the theoretical scheme we may hypothesize that the high-skill employees will be more directed toward maturity than the low-skill employees.

Evidence for Hypothesis XIII. Let us begin with the last prediction first. If the prediction is valid, then the employees in subsystem A should aspire more toward the mature ends of the continua than will the employees in subsystem B (Plant Y). Let us first examine the dimensions of individual aspiration. In Table 9 certain dimensions of the employees' self-concept in A and B (Plant Y) are examined and as expected more employees in A express aspirations that are toward the mature end of the continua than do employees from B. Conversely, more employees in B express aspirations that are toward the immature end of the continua than do employees in A.

TABLE 9

DIMENSIONS OF SELF-CONCEPT OF EMPLOYEES
IN SUBSYSTEM A AND B (PLANT Y)
Expressed in Per Cent

	A(N = 30)	B(N = 30)	Stat. Sig.
1. I feel I have nothing to offer. I am not worth much................................30		50	.0582
2. I feel I have much to offer. I have a high regard for myself..................60		33	.0192
3. I prefer to be passive, to be the recipient of someone else's directions..........20		70	>.0001
4. I prefer to direct people, to initiate action...50		00	>.0001
5. I aspire for high-quality performance.....53		00	>.0001

Now that we have established that more employees in subsystem A than B aspire toward the mature ends of the continua, and if as the framework predicts the employees in subsystem A are more frustrated than the employees in subsystem B, then on the basis of our theoretical propositions we predict:

1. The absenteeism in Plant Y will tend to be higher in subsystem A and lower in B and/or
2. The turnover will tend to be higher in subsystem A than B and/or
3. The expression of "pent up tension influencing outside activities" will be higher in subsystem A than B and/or

4. The quality of production will be relatively lower in subsystem A than B and/or

5. The need for unionization will be higher in subsystem A than B and

6. All of the predicted changes will be greater in Plant Y than in Plant X.

Let us turn to see if the data fit the hypotheses.

1. The personnel records of Plant Y show that for the period of the research the absenteeism figures are in the direction that is predicted for the two departments. In subsystem A the absenteeism is 3.6 per cent and 3.9 per cent. In B the figures for the two departments are 3 per cent and 3.2 per cent.

2. The problem is more complex when we consider turnover. The turnover figures (for the same period) for the two departments in subsystem A are 7.3 per cent and 21.7 per cent. The turnover figures for the two departments in subsystem B are 15.7 per cent and 16.4 per cent. Thus we find that in one department of A the figures are higher as predicted. This is not the case for the other department. Why?

We can state some hypotheses which of course would require further research to test. If we may assume that leaving the organization is a more drastic adaptive mechanism than being absent, then some possible reasons become evident. In both departments (subsystem A) the wages are high. The employee may earn high wages if he "makes out" in piecework. In order to "make out" the employee must learn the skills that are necessary. An analysis of the turnover in the department with the turnover figure of 21.7 per cent suggests that *all* the men who left were men who after a few months apprenticeship decided that they would never be able to make out and asked to be transferred to another department or left the factory. Thus the turnover figure (although) in the predicted direction does not really support the hypothesis. In fact, among the regular employees in A, turnover is less than in B. It is our hypothesis that since the employees in subsystem A are highly skilled and highly paid, they will not find it convenient to leave the plant, rather they should adapt to the pressure either by greater absenteeism (which is the case) and/or by increased

Well, there's not much to say. When I go home, I'm bushed. You know, when you're pent up all during the day, you just feel as though you're knocked out. And I go home and I sleep. Sometimes when I can get up in time, I might go out to a few clubs or go visiting with the family. But I'm dead tired during the evening.

6. Finally, we turn to the hypothesis that absenteeism, turnover, quality, and unionization should be greater problems in Plant Y than in X. The reader will recall that because Plant X's turnover and absenteeism are so low no figures are kept. We may only conjecture since the need exists in Plant Y to keep the figures, the absenteeism, and turnover are higher.

Turning to the quality, the figures are clearly in line with the hypothesis since all of the appropriate figures in Plant X are in the plus category whereas none are in the plus category in Plant Y. Perhaps the best indication is that the upper management agree that Plant Y has greater quality problems than does Plant X. As to unionization, the figures again support the hypothesis. Less than 1 per cent of the employees in Plant X report that they desire a union ($>.0001$).

Hypothesis XIV: The Competition and Rivalry Will Be Greater, and the Friendship Less in Subsystem A than in Subsystem B (Plant Y). We have shown that as the pressure is increased by management to decrease costs, errors, back work, and as the opportunity to have a kitty is decreased, the employees will tend to place greater emphasis on "making a fair day's pay" every day. This follows because without the kitty they do not have anything to fall back on in case they are given "tough" jobs to produce (i.e., jobs whose piece rates, in the eyes of the employees, are low). It is important to emphasize that everytime a piece-rate employee comes to work he has the anxiety if he will be able to make a "day's pay" during that day. We recall that 52 per cent of the employees report that their rates are "low" or "some low, some high." This gives us some idea of the degree of uncertainty that the employee experiences. With the kitty his anxiety over uncertainty is greatly diminished. Without it, it is increased.

It follows that there should be increased competition among the employees for the "easy" jobs (which increase the probability of "making out"). This competition should lead to interpersonal rivalry and hostility.

If the above is valid, then the increase in interpersonal rivalry and hostility should be greater in subsystem A than in B (Y) because the kitties (in A) have been almost completely eliminated and it is in A that the IBM system has taken control of whatever small kitty is permitted. Another reason why the hostility should be greater in subsystem A than B is that the kitty is (as is already pointed out) lower in subsystem B. Therefore, employees in subsystem B have less to lose from the loss of the kitty.

Evidence for Hypothesis XIV. The data confirm the hypothesis. Seventy-one per cent of employees in subsystem B report that people are friendly whereas only 30 per cent in A report the same (.0008). The corollary question is also in the same direction. Whereas only 20 per cent of the employees in B report "unfriendly" employees, 70 per cent of the employees in A report the same ($>.0001$).

Moreover, when one questions the employees who report unfriendliness, the overwhelming majority describe it in terms of rivalry induced by piecework.

Oh, I think it has changed quite a bit. In the old plant there was much more friendliness. Now the prices are getting tighter and the fellows are squabbling among each other. Also in the old plant there were more ways of skinning a cat and making a buck. Things are tightening up now and you can't make a buck as easily. They're kind of putting the squeeze on I guess—something maybe they have to do to keep the company going.

Well, I think it could be improved, it's not too good. I'm a fine guy really to talk about this because I've just blew my stack yesterday about something. You know in piecework you get jobs sometimes that aren't well timed and some are well timed and you always wonder, are you getting your share of the easy jobs or are you getting your share of the tough jobs. I have the feeling, and I think some of the other fellows feel that the jobs aren't passed out honestly and fairly.

I'll tell you what I think—I think most men would prefer to have a real honest to goodness time study. One that we could really do the job and alleviate any dissension because then there wouldn't be easy jobs and tough jobs.

I'll tell you, Mister, I told you before that I didn't have a goal, but if I could do something to bring back morale the way it used to be, I'd really work hard. But I don't think you can, and believe me they're making more money than they ever made before, God, they're making more money; but today you may give him $3.25 and the only thing he wants is $3.50; and give him $3.50 and the only thing he wants is $3.75. Once in awhile you talk to them about the good old days when people were friendly, and they laugh at you. It's as if, you know, that isn't important any more.

More evidence is found when we analyze the reasons employees give for "low morale." We note that of those employees in B who feel their departments have low morale only 25 per cent attribute it to "competition for easy jobs." Of those employees in A who feel their departments have low morale, 59 per cent attribute it to the competition among employees for the easy jobs (.0045).

Hypothesis XV: Plant X Will Have Less Employee Rivalry than Plant Y. Since we have shown that Plant Y reports more pressure than Plant X, and since we have demonstrated (hypothesis XIV) that the degree of friendship is related to the pressure, we predict that the reported friendship should be higher in subsystem A and B in Plant X than in subsystem A and B in Plant Y. Moreover, we can predict that the differences in reported friendship should be greater between the subsystem A's in Plant X and Y. Since the degree of friendship is related to the degree of pressure, it also follows that the reported friendship should be higher in subsystem A and B in Plant X than in subsystem A and B in Plant Y and that the differences should be greater between the subsystem A's in Plant X and Y.

Evidence for Hypothesis XV. The data are presented in Table 11. They confirm the hypotheses. Subsystem A and B in Plant X report greater degree of friendliness than do subsystem A and B in Plant Y. Moreover the differences are greater between subsystem A in Plant X and Y.

To summarize, we predict that as the pressure from management increases, the employees will not tend to combat the pressure as a cohesive group because their culture rewards apathy, noninvolvement, and togetherness; none of which are norms upon which cohesive groups can be based. Moreover, we predict

TABLE 11

COMPARISON OF FRIENDSHIP
SCORES IN SUBSYSTEM A AND B, PLANT X AND Y
Expressed in Per Cent

	SUBSYSTEM A			SUBSYSTEM B		
	Plant X(N = 34)	Plant Y(N = 30)	Stat. Sig.	Plant X(N = 90)	Plant Y(N = 30)	Stat. Sig.
People are friendly....	90	30	>.0001	90	71	.0062
People are unfriendly..	10	00	>.0001	10	20	.0793*

* Not significant.

further that one reaction of the employees will be to place greater emphasis on "making a fair day's pay" every day. This new emphasis will increase competition for the "easy jobs" and consequently increases the interpersonal rivalry among the employees. This, in turn, will act to further weaken the probability of cohesive groups to combat management pressure.

We conclude that the Plant Y social system induces greater tension, conflict, frustration, than does the Plant X social system. The degree of self-actualization, therefore, in Y should be less than in X and within Y it should be less in subsystem A. The data (Table 12) confirm the hypothesis.

TABLE 12

FREQUENCY DISTRIBUTION OF HIGH * AND LOW SELF-
ACTUALIZATION SCORES IN PLANT X AND Y
Expressed in Per Cent

	PLANT X		PLANT Y	
	A(N = 34)	B(N = 90)	A(N = 30)	B(N = 30)
High............	88	84	57	77
Low............	12	14	43	23

* The cut-off point used is the same as that used in our other industrial organization studies to predict absenteeism, turnover, etc. High is 70–100 and low is less than 70.

The employees in Y, who tend to be further along the maturity scales than are Plant X employees, react by internalizing some of the pressure and by a higher degree of (a) absenteeism, (b) desire for unionization, (c) hostility against middle management, and (*d*) a decrease in the quality of their work. Because of (*a*) the sanctions imposed by the informal culture, (*b*) the already established relationships with the management, the employees in Y do not express the tension and resentment openly toward management.

CHAPTER

VI

Some Unanswered Issues

Up to this point the objective of this book has been to outline in somewhat systematic detail the methodological specifics and the theoretical underpinnings (such as they exist at this time) of *one* approach to the study of human behavior in organizations.

As has been repeatedly stressed, the point of view is by no means a mature one. Many key questions remain unanswered or at best only partially discussed. Much more knowledge is required. For example, what are the precise criteria that one may use to know when he has discovered (or conceptually reconstructed by the use of the model) the pattern of the relevant variables that is assumed to be the organization in the empirical world? What specific operational definitions are there available to the researcher to show him when the model adequately represents the organization as a whole?

Another important unresolved issue is the problem of defining the behavioral content of the "parts" in the model. In Figure 2, pages 82–83, for example, one finds two types of parts. First are those such as "intake process," "fair incentive system," "kitty," "informal employee world," etc. Second, are the lines which represent the process by which one (or a set of variables) leads to another (or set of variables). Thus the variables in subsystem A and B are depicted as leading to a particular set of predispositions and these in turn lead to simplified but satisfied employees, etc. Not only must the behavioral content of each circle be clearly defined but the process depicted by the lines must be made explicit.

How precisely (what behavioral mechanisms are involved) do the four major predispositions become the informal employee culture? How precisely does the informal employee culture lead to employee satisfaction? How does passive foremanship lead to the psychological contract? How does management satisfaction feed back to reinforce the input process?

Still another question that seems crucial is related to the assertion often made in this analysis that the system is self-maintaining; i.e., its predisposition is not to change (as long as the environment does not change significantly). This assertion implies a tolerance for balance *within* each part and *among* the parts that constitute the whole. If this assertion is to be tested then the tolerances for balance within each, and among the parts must be made explicit. The actual behavior mechanisms that form and maintain the tolerance levels require explication. It would be especially important to define the tolerances in quantified terms.

Finally, an approach that claims to aspire to be scientific inquiry cannot be satisfied with the understanding to consider only a specific case. Consequently, it is important if this approach is found useful to enumerate the types of questions that it purports to deal with. What kinds of generalizations is it hoping to generate? What is its universe of discourse?

The task to answer these questions has only begun. In the next few pages the writer outlines some of his thoughts that have evolved from his research experiences to date. The discussion is presented to indicate the direction in which the writer is going at the present time.

Some Operational Criteria for the Study of the Organization as a Whole

A crucial question that must be answered concretely if the methodology presented here is to be operationally meaningful is how does one know if and when he has enumerated all the relevant variables and their interrelationships? At the moment the writer has only a few rather crude and simple criteria to offer. They are by no means inclusive or exclusive. They are rather suggestive of the direction that may be fruitful.

a) The first (simple) test is to ask the obvious question if all the data that have been obtained empirically are accounted for, i.e., if their place in the pattern has been ascertained. For example, in Plant X all the data that we uncovered have been included in the analysis (see Figure 2, pages 82–83). No residual categories remain.

This criteria is a dangerous one if used by itself. It is not enough to feel confident in the method simply because all the data obtained have been accounted for. The difficulty is that the researcher tends to discover those data that are required by his theoretical framework. Thus to say that one has discovered the whole pattern *because* no residual data remain may simply mean that the theoretical scheme one used is limited. All that one really uncovers is that which the theoretical framework permits. The probability (especially at this early stage) that the framework is incomplete is quite high. Consequently, further criteria are needed to increase our confidence that all the relevant variables have been ascertained.

b) A second criterion is related to the assumption that a system is self-maintaining. One might require the researcher to enumerate and describe the behavioral mechanisms or processes by which the system is self-maintaining. If, for example, a pattern is ascertained but no feedback processes can be described (or at least hypothesized) whereby the self-maintenance processes of the system are explicit, then the probability is high that the total system has not been uncovered. There are more variables to be found.

c) But accounting for the self-maintenance processes of a system is still not adequate. It is quite possible for the researcher to describe a pattern of parts and account for their maintenance as a whole and still not have discovered all the relevant variables. The researcher may simply have studied a subsystem of the whole which by itself is self-maintaining.

d) In order to increase one's confidence in the inclusiveness of the analyses, the researcher could be required to make predictions about the behavior of the system that might occur in the future, especially behavior that is not a part of the present analysis.

There are several levels of prediction that one might hypothesize. The simplest would be to predict the stability of the system over time. One may hypothesize, for example, that five years later if no external environmental factors can be shown to have influenced the system, it will not tend to change.[1]

Another level of prediction would be to predict the impact of changes upon the system that occur while the researcher is conducting his study which are unexpected and not part of the original research design. The "de-skilling" of the jobs mentioned in Chapter III is an example. Although the researcher was permitted to have no control over the nature of the change or its introduction into the system, he was able to observe it and state some a priori hypotheses regarding the reactions of the highly skilled employees to changes.

Still another level of prediction would be the impact of a known change to be instituted in the organization at a *future* date. For example, new budgetary control systems are being instituted in Plant X (some have already been installed). The researcher could make predictions about the impact of these controls *before* they are introduced into the system. This has been partially attempted in a qualitative and preliminary manner primarily for the foremen and somewhat for the employees and top management (see previous chapter). A sign of a more rigorous analysis would be, of course, if the researcher could specify specifically the nature and the degree of impact that the controls will have upon *each* part of the whole as well as the whole.

An even more rigorous type of prediction would be to stipulate the "path of impact" of the new budgetary controls throughout the system. Such a prediction would include the time dimension. One would be able to predict when and where the "path of impact" will begin, its intensity, as well as its future course.

Defining the Behavioral Correlates of the Parts

Another important unanswered set of questions is related to the requirement that the researcher describe as accurately as pos-

---

[1] Such an hypothesis is illustrated crudely in an article by the author entitled, "Some Problems in Conceptualizing Organizational Climate," *Administrative Science Quarterly*, Vol. II, No. 4 (March, 1958).

sible the nature of each part of the system in behavioral terms. Such a description would include the behavioral content of each part, the objective it plays as a part, the relationship of its objectives to the objectives of the immediately surrounding parts and to the whole. To use a medical analogy, it is not only important to know the relationship of the liver to the whole body, but one ought to specify the nature of the liver. These two criteria are, in fact, inseparable. One cannot really understand the liver without understanding the whole body and vice versa.

One word of caution to the researcher who prefers to include in his model only parts that are on a similar level of analysis. In the writer's experience focusing on the organization (i.e., pattern as a whole) brings together variables that are traditionally kept in separate levels of analyses (e.g., variables on the individual, small group, cultural levels of analyses). This may make the researcher who prefers to include in his analysis variables on the same level quite uncomfortable. It may give him the feeling of being less systematic and "neat."

In some way this is true. Multilevel variable analysis, at this time, will tend to be less rigorous. However, a plea is made for the respect of the nature of organization. Typically the parts that comprise it are not ordered according to traditional academic departmental lines. A different concept of rigor may be required. It may be that in these studies one is being "tough-minded" when one is able to interrelate variables on different levels of analyses into a whole rather than to separate them into their appropriate academic categories of analysis.

Another aspect of the problem of defining the behavioral correlates of the parts is related to the feedback and "feed upon" mechanism. For example, in Figure 2 certain parts are shown to evolve from others. Thus "management satisfaction" results from (feeds upon) the outputs of the "informal employee culture." "Passive foremen" also results from the same part. "Management satisfaction" on the other hand also feeds back to support and maintain the "hiring process" which in turn results in two work worlds, etc.

If the analytical method proposed is to aspire to respectable rigor, then the exact behavioral manifestations of the "feed-back" and "feed-upon" processes must be made explicit. For example, how does the management satisfaction result from the employee culture? This question is not answered in the present analysis. Also unanswered is how does the management satisfaction feed back to reinforce and maintain the hiring process and what specific behavior is contained in this feedback process?

Has the Degree of Disturbance That Any Part Can Experience without Influencing Its Relationships with the Other Parts and the Whole Been Made Explicit?

A third unanswered question is related to the assumption that the basic predisposition of the system is to maintain itself. The question arises, how is this done? How does the system prevent or resist change? What is the system's "change tolerance?"

If, as required above, accurate descriptions are available of the pattern, the nature of each part and the feedback and feed-upon processes, then the degree of tolerance to change of the system would not be difficult to ascertain. One could hopefully measure the "change tolerance" of the whole by measuring the amount of change *in* any given part or any *relationship among* parts that would make *no* significant difference to the whole. In this analysis one would be interested in the pressures toward change that do not affect the total pattern.

Another required study (one that is more common) would be to measure the points where a change within any given part, or among a subset of parts, makes a difference to the whole. This research would complement the one described above.

A third type of study would be to ascertain the degree of disturbance that occurs. The object would be to study how deep or strong is the disturbance, how long it exists, the paths required to return the system to a steady state, and the new pattern required to maintain the new state of affairs.

One further word about how a disturbance might be quantified. The prediction of a disturbance we note above requires insight into the tolerance for change *within* any given part as well as the tolerance for change in the *interrelationships among* the parts. If this is the case, then one might conceive of the following states of an organization's tolerance for change.

1. *High* tolerance to change *within* a given part—*high* tolerance to change *between* parts.
2. *High* tolerance . . . *within* a given part—*low* tolerance . . . *between* parts.
3. *Low* tolerance . . . *within* a given part—*high* tolerance . . . *between* parts.
4. *Low* tolerance . . . *within* a given part—*low* tolerance . . . *between* parts.

State one (high-high) would represent the case of maximum resistance to change while state four the minimum resistance to change. State one may be an example of a system with "over rigidity" while state four an example of a system being "too easily influenced." [2]

The Nature of the Questions Asked by the Approach

It might be helpful to differentiate the boundaries of the universe being considered by defining some typical questions that might be considered central to what has been called *organizational behavior:*

1. How (by what processes) do human (or social) organizations arise? What is the "pace" of their birth? Do they evolve over time? Do they develop suddenly? Slowly? Are both possibilities possible? If so, under what conditions will organizations evolve and under what conditions will they be suddenly developed?

2. By what processes do organizations grow? Is the pattern of organizational growth "inherent" in the nature of organization? How much is it influenced by external factors?

3. How do organizations maintain themselves internally and still adapt to the external environment in which they are imbedded? By what processes do organizations significantly alter the environment? Also, by what processes does the environment significantly alter the internal make-up of the organization?

[2] For an interesting recent discussion on this problem see Alvin W. Gouldner, "Organizational Analysis," R. K. Merton, L. Broom, and L. S. Cottrell, Jr. (eds.), *Sociology Today* (New York: Basic Books, Inc., 1959), pp. 419–23.

4. Does the nature of organizational objectives influence significantly the creation, growth, and self-maintenance of the organization?

5. Are there generalizations possible regarding the processes of organization construction and disintegration? Is it possible (and fruitful) to conceive of criteria for "healthy" or "effective" organization as well as "unhealthy" or "ineffective" organization for "tired," "run-down," "anemic," etc., organizations? If so, does it mean that one might be able to define when "chemotherapy" is needed and when "surgery" is required? What would "organizational rest" be? What would organizational stress look like.[3]

6. Are there generalizations possible regarding the patterns of organization? For example are the possible number of significantly different patterns finite or infinite? If they are finite what knowledge is necessary to discover the total possible number of cases? If they are infinite, then what possibilities for scientific generalizations exist?

7. Are there generalizations possible regarding the nature of parts when they are "organic" parts? For example, many individual personalities are part of an organization. Is it possible that the very nature of organization coerces "different" people to behave relatively alike? If so, would this lead to generalizations regarding the probable range of "styles of living" within an organization? Similarly are there generalizations possible regarding the nature and function of informal groups and of norms when they are (organic) parts of an organization.

8. What is the nature of organizational cohesiveness? How can it be measured? What inhibits and what facilitates organizational cohesiveness? What is the relation between (various degrees of) organizational cohesiveness and organizational effectiveness?

9. Finally, much research is required to ascertain if there are any generalizations possible about behavior that characterizes "feed-upon" and behavior that characterizes "feedback" processes. To put it another way, is there something in the nature

---

[3] Hans Selye suggests that it is meaningful to speak of a general stress syndrome. *The Stress of Life* (New York: McGraw-Hill Book Co., Inc., 1956).

of "feedback" processes that will behaviorally differentiate them from the "feed-upon" processes.

The questions above focus on the organization as a whole. Very little is asked about its environment. The omission of the environment does not imply that organizations are relatively closed systems unaffected by their environments. Nothing could be further from the truth. Organizations are open systems continually influencing and being influenced by the environment. The lack of discussion of this very crucial area is due to the writer's limitations. He finds it difficult enough to study organizations as a whole, no less to focus with equal rigor upon the organization-environment problems. It is acknowledged, however, that a complete organizational theory will require that the organizational and environmental studies be integrated.

CHAPTER

VII

The Usefulness of the Organizational Analysis to the Practitioner

LET US NOW turn our attention to the practical usefulness of the research. What can an organization learn from such research? What value can it have to the employees and management? Below are a few suggestions obtained from an analysis of the transcripts and notes taken at feedback sessions and from interviews with the various levels of management.

"It Provides an Analysis That Is (in One Sense) Timeless"

The feedback sessions usually begin with a report of the (quantitative) results for each question. The questions are usually grouped according to topic headings (e.g., employee-management relations, employee morale, job satisfaction, feelings about the company, etc.). Following this descriptive presentation (or interspersed at relevant places) the analyst usually raises questions about patterns that may begin to appear.

The second step, and a most important one, is the feedback of the model (as shown in Figure 2, pages 82–83). Here the researcher takes a position that the pattern or positioning of the factors as shown in Figure 2 will not change by their own accord. To put it another way, it is predicted that if there are quantitative changes in any of the variables, they will be so minor that they will not influence the system significantly.

The research conducted during the second phase suggests

some further (and perhaps more basic) values of the model to the practitioner). We recall that the researcher, by using the model is able to state some valid predictions about the impact of, and the path for change within, the organization. The researcher is able to predict (and apparently at times more accurately than management) such phenomena as the departments that

1. Will feel the greatest pressure and least pressure from the change;
2. Will react to the change by absenteeism, turnover, and those that will not;
3. Will decrease the quality of work and those that will not;
4. Will desire to unionize and those that will not.

Would it not be possible and useful for organizations to have ongoing research teams to develop a similar model for their plant's social system? The model would be continually revised and made more valid while at the same time it would serve as basis from which to make predictions about such things as (1) the future state of the social system, (2) probable impact of various changes being considered, (3) probable reactive mechanisms that will tend to be employed by employees in different departments, by foremen, by the manager, etc.

Such a program would not be difficult to develop nor expensive to maintain. In a plant up to two thousand employees, one senior person with an assistant and appropriate secretarial help could accomplish the task without difficulty. This team would spend their time conducting long-range studies.

It would be crucial that the research team not be used (in the usual sense of a staff team) to suggest possible courses of action and to make recommendations. Such a role would tend to inhibit the probability that they will gain the confidences of the individual respondents. The professional role of this small team would have to be worked out meticulously. The benefits, to *all* the participants, could be many. An important contribution to organizational theory could also be made.

"It Organizes Our Thoughts"
Perhaps the most frequently mentioned value by top executives is that the model presents them with a valuable convenient map

of a very complex world. One executive describes it as follows, "I feel with it I can get above the trees and see the whole forest. It gives me some semblance of the whole organization as well as some idea of its depth." Another states, "Much of what you presented I have felt intuitively for years. The framework helps to make sense out of the whole thing. For me this (Figure 2) is the first snapshot of our company that gives me an idea of what makes this place tick."

Thus, as in the case of the researcher, a most important value of the model is its capacity to organize that which is intuitively known.

"It Provides Insights into the 'Why' and Simultaneously Saves Us Money"

A third value of the analysis reported by management is that it provides them with some insight into *why* things occur as they do. For example, it helps to show management that the low turnover, low absenteeism, etc., are resultants of the employees' actualization or satisfaction primarily of four predispositions: wages and job security; togetherness; control; and noninvolvement, which are so pervasive that they may also be viewed as the norms of the informal employee world. The lack of a union in Plant X is related to the high congruency between what the employees report they want to actualize while at work and the demands of the organization. Similarly the low desire for upward mobility and the lack of involvement in the formal aspects of the company is also related to the relatively high possibility for self-actualization. The validity of these conclusions is enhanced by the study of Plant Y. There, the desire for unionization, upward mobility are greater and the lack of involvement is *less* because of the decrease in the probability of individual self-actualization.

Such insights may help management to realize the pitfalls in spending thousands of dollars attempting to influence the employees to identify with the company through the use of various "selling" programs. In Plant X and Y high production exists, partially because the employees do *not* feel they must identify with the company. They believe it is management's job to worry about the company, and they appreciate the wonderful job management is doing. It is precisely because management is doing such a good job that the employees remain loyal to the company. From their point of view their apathy is a sign of loyalty!

If these results are valid then how valid would it be for management to assume that there is something wrong or bad in the employees' apparent disinterest in the plant and the economic workings of the free enterprise system? Would not courses in economics etc., be at best a waste of money and at worst, a hostile act from the employees' point of view? The employees' lack of interest in the workings of the free enterprise system stems (in their opinion) from their faith in the competence of the top management.[1]

On the other hand, the employees are not completely ignorant of the requirements of the free market system. They are keen to sense the impact of supply and demand upon their jobs. They are so well aware of the impact of competition, the reader may recall, that some of the highest skilled craftsmen accept the change as part of the fact of life. As one said, "Where would the company be if they didn't meet the price of our competitors?" Moreover, they seem to believe in the importance of restricting production. This implies that they must hold some hypotheses about the workings of the economic system.

The research also helps by providing evidence that elaborate communication programs, expensive newspapers, pamphlets, etc., to enthuse the employees with the company are unnecessary and could lead to negative results.

Still another practical question the research raises is the probable value of instituting courses in creativity or having "brainstorming" sessions. Would such measures influence the basic nature of the systems which, as they stand now, inhibit employee and foremen creativity.

The research also raises practical questions about the desire of some managers to introduce foreman training especially in human relations and leadership. The data suggest that the foremen feel

---

[1] The writer is reporting the employees' point of view of courses in economics and not his own.

that human relations training for them is unnecessary, irrelevant, and annoying. The foremen believe they are effective if they adhere to the psychological work contract. Instilling them with all sorts of complex human relations behavioral skills without instituting basic changes in Plant X and Y's systems could lead to real difficulties.[2] Skills as sensitivity, listening, helping employees express their emotions in their plant culture could get the foremen into much trouble. Any leadership style that attempts to deal with them on a deeper interpersonal level (although, in the long run, might be healthier) would indeed be greeted with caution and confusion, if not open hostility.

Moreover, one can imagine the frustration of the foremen if they are told to take a course designed to help them become "more effective leaders." First, they will soon realize that they can use little if anything of what they learn in the course. Second, given to the mood they are in, they may feel hurt by, and hostile toward, the management, for implying that the solution to their problems is training.

The analysis also provides insight into the roots of the lack of desire on the part of many employees to become foremen. The employees' lack of desire to be a foreman is not seen as disloyalty or indifference to the company. On the contrary, from their point of view they are being deeply loyal. They sense the few opportunities for advancement that exist and rather than (as one said) "raise hell, we say to hell with going up. We're here to make a buck."

Still another value of the research is that it raises questions about the possibility being presently considered by management to place the foremen on an incentive system in order to increase their effectiveness. The problem of foremen effectiveness is not caused by the lack of motivation on the part of the foremen. The foremen's behavior is highly influenced by the psychological contract on the one hand and by the pressure, undercutting, and low status of their jobs on the other. One can raise serious questions

---

[2] For some interesting studies see, A. Zalesnik, *Foreman Training in a Growing Enterprise* (Boston: Division of Research, Harvard Business School, 1951); and Frank Jasinski, "The Dynamics of Organizational Behavior," *Personnel,* Vol. XXXVI, No. 2 (March–April, 1959), pp. 60–67.

about the value of trying to pay foremen more money if the basic nature of the system in which they exist is not changed. In fact, one may predict that, at the moment, the foremen believe they deserve increases in wages, basically, as a reward for their *dissatisfaction*. Such motivation for higher wages is not necessarily going to lead to more effective foremenship—in the sense that management thinks of the term "effective." Moreover, as the analysis points out, the system "simplifies" the foremen. To pay them more in order to act as if they are "more enriched," does not seem to be realistic.

In diagnosing the foremen as "simplified" and "frustrated" the researcher is making inferences about the psychological state of the foremen that may go beyond the complete conscious awareness of most of the foremen. If these inferences are valid, then policies could be inferred from them that would lead management to take action which is in the best interests of the foremen but which the foremen would not see in the same manner. For example, the majority of the foremen would definitely vote for an incentive system. However, as suggested above, the establishment of a supervisory incentive system is not necessarily a helpful policy for the foremen or for the organization.

"It Provides a Realistic Basis for Executive Development"

If the system of Plant X remains as is, few of the top executives will come from the ranks. Probably most will come from university graduates, who no doubt will serve lengthy apprenticeships "on the line."

The development of executives in this plant will require a unique training experience. Their course of executive development along with the traditional subjects, will need to offer the future executive insights into how to deal with people who feel a low sense of self-worth; who are apathetic, and who are loyal to the company basically because they do *not* have to worry about it. According to this analysis many of these employees have accepted a state of being dependent and submissive upon the management. If this is valid, then the top leadership must be cautious in their dealing with the employees who are apathetic and have a low sense of self-worth. They can be easily irritated especially by leaders who try to instill in them the same enthusiasm and motivation that they (the leaders) have.

The leaders will also need to develop insights into their own selves. They need to understand their impatience with people who seem, to them, not to have the degree of enthusiam, directiveness, productivity, and desire for upward mobility that they have. They will have to be helped to realize that dealing with these workers by labeling them as "lazy," "irresponsible," "disloyal" is not only ineffective but fundamentally hostile. Such labeling misses completely the possibility that the employees have (unconsciously) decided that they can best adapt to the organization and give it its desired production at lowest cost by becoming apathetic and alienated!

Along with providing insight into some of the basic problems of executive development, the research can help to provide suggestions for the first step in the executives' development. First, many of the corporate executives remarked that the discussion of the feedback results provide a rich source of material for many discussions on all levels in the company. What better way, suggests one executive, to develop ourselves and our leadership abilities than by using ourselves as our case study.

The president and a few of the corporate officers discovered a second way in which the research could help them in their own development. During the feedback session one of the researchers observed the reactions of the group. An analysis of these observations showed, among other things, that over 95 per cent of the discussion was conducted by the president and the vice-president in charge of manufacturing. In all cases when the plant managers spoke, it was in reply to a question by these two and top executives.

These and other similar results, lead the researcher to raise the question about the degree of freedom the plant managers feel to speak as they please and to explore problems openly in front of the top management. At the outset the president replied that there was certainly no problem of the plant managers "cowing" to the top executive. However, when the vice-president arrived at the meeting and was told of the researchers' inference he agreed with the researcher. This lead to a lively discussion which terminated with the president suggesting that it might be valuable if a study were conducted of the top-management group. The researcher agreed.

"It Provides Knowledge upon Which to Plan Impact of Future Changes"

It is possible, from the analysis presented, to derive effective policies and practices with which to introduce changes and to predict the probable impact of changes upon the various segments of the organization. Thus, in making the changes in the high-skill department reported in the previous chapter, it is clear that the latest suggestions of some behavioral scientists, such as to involve employees in the change through participation, could lead to unexpected difficulties. As has been shown, in this company, changes can be instituted quite effectively with almost no participation by the employees as long as the new wages are as high or higher than the ones received on the previous jobs. This insight is not completely new for the management. They followed such a procedure before they ever received the analysis above. (The most the analysis did do was to provide the management with some insight into why their practices worked.)

However, the same may not be said about the introduction of the budget system into the plant. Here the management feels that the analysis has brought to them insights which they did not have before. The executives in the controllers office as well as those on the line are now more aware of the possible impact of the budgets upon the foremen and the employees and can consider other steps to lessen any disturbance.

The Long-Range Effectiveness of Management Philosophy

Is the present management policy the best one for the company to have to meet the challenges of the future? More specifically, does the policy of minimal pressure, high wages, excellent benefits, and excellent working conditions provide the best bases for future growth in an increasingly competitive society?

Some insights into the question can be obtained by permitting Plant X to represent the "older" philosophy of minimal pressure and Plant Y the "newer" philosophy of increased pressure to cut costs, errors, etc. Then the differences found to exist between Plants X and Y can be viewed as a map of the changes the entire corporation will experience as it increases its uses of the more pressure oriented philosophy.

If our data are valid, then we can state the following conclusions.

1. The policy of minimal pressure and "be nice" to the employees will tend to show few human or production problems as long as no new demands are made upon the organization. In short, as long as organizational stability is possible and/or valued over growth.

2. Stability, however, does not tend to be tolerable to a management whose basic philosophy is to grow and develop. Plant X and Y's corporate management holds to the "grow or die" philosophy.

3. Consequently, Plant X can never rest on its laurels. It will always be asked to find new ways to cut and control costs. On the basis of our study of Plant Y, we conclude that under pressure for cost reduction the following will tend to occur in a company like Plant X.

   a) Since high-skill and low-skill employees are not accustomed to pressure, they will tend to resent it even though by the standards of other plants the amount of pressure is small.

   b) The resentment will be higher in the high-skill departments and lower in the low-skill departments.

   c) Low-skill and high-skill employees will not tend to express their resentments openly in front of management or the foremen.

   d) Low-skill and high-skill employees will tend to project most of the blame for their tension on the middle management.

   e) The middle management will not feel understood by top management. They will tend to react by increasing the pressure downward.

   f) Since the foremen view themselves as being second-rate, their tendency will be to coerce the middle management to take on the responsibility for the pressure.

   g) The top management will tend to require that the middle management "carry the ball" for the pressure because they do not tend to have confidence in the foremen.

h) Self-inflicted pressure to "make out" every day will increase especially among high-skill employees.

i) The quality of work will decrease especially among the high-skill employees.

j) Competition and rivalry among employees will increase and friendliness will decrease.

k) Employees will find it difficult to create cohesive informal groups.

l) The more mature employees will tend to increase their desire for unionization, be absent more frequently, quit in greater numbers, and find it more difficult to achieve their own production standards.

The resultants above will tend to make the management more anxious and apprehensive. Consequently they will tend to increase the pressure on the middle and first-line supervisors. The pressure in turn will be passed down to the employee especially by the middle-management supervisor who will find himself increasingly doing the work normally expected of a foreman. The increased pressure on the employees will only tend to increase the employees' resentment; and consequently, decrease quality, increase production costs, increase absenteeism, turnover, and increase the employee's need for a strong union. As these increase, management will tend to apply new pressure and create new and tighter controls. The loop is then closed because the increased pressure will only tend to compound the problems that we mention above.

We have arrived at the end of the present research only to see more clearly how important it is to emphasize that the above represents primarily an interim report of work in progress. Much more research needs to be conducted before the value of the approach can be evaluated.

Perhaps for management the most important value of the research at this time is expressed by the president when he said that the research helped him to see even more clearly how complex and difficult it is to truly understand human behavior in an organization.

Index

175

*This book has been set on the Linotype in
11 point Times Roman leaded 2 points.
Chapter numbers are in 14 point Times
Roman caps with 18 point Caslon Open
roman numerals. Chapter titles are in 24
point Nicholas Cochin caps and lower case.
The size of the type page is 25 by 42 picas.*